From Narrative Onward

Writing With Focus

As part of Houghton Mifflin's ongoing
commitment to the environment, this text
has been printed on recycled paper.

From Narrative Onward

WRITING WITH FOCUS

Diane Fitton
Monroe Community College

Barbara Warner
Monroe Community College

HOUGHTON MIFFLIN COMPANY   Boston   New York

Senior Sponsoring Editor: Mary Jo Southern
Associate Editor: Kellie Cardone
Editorial Associate: Danielle Richardson
Senior Project Editor: Fred Burns
Production/Design Coordinator: Jodi O'Rourke
Manufacturing Manager: Florence Cadran
Senior Marketing Manager: Nancy Lyman

Cover design: Dutton & Sherman Design
Cover image: © Kevin N. Ghiglione/SIS

Acknowledgments for reprinted materials appear on page 277.

Printed in the U.S.A.

Library of Congress Catalog Card Number: 00-133907

ISBN: 0-618-00491-2

1 2 3 4 5 6 7 8 9—DOC—04 03 02 01 00

CONTENTS

PART THREE

Language Supplement 241

PREFACE

This text evolved from a series of exercises for students in developmental composition classes. Working together on these classroom materials, we realized that because of our pedagogical backgrounds and experience, a total of more than forty years in the classroom, we had come to a similar perspective about how to engage students in the writing process. The next step was to share our approach with other students and instructors. The result of this effort is *From Narrative Onward.*

From Narrative Onward is predicated on several assumptions about its audience. One is that most adult learners enrolled in a developmental composition course have a wealth of personal experience to share but need abundant practice with writing as a tool for communication. Consequently, the materials included in the textbook are based on familiar themes of human existence. Readings by professional writers introduce each theme; follow-up questions and topics encourage responses from life experience. Writing about what they know, students are freed to focus on composition technique. Models of each phase of the writing process reinforce instruction and inspire confidence.

A second assumption is that students, whether they are newly learning the skills of composition or merely filling in gaps in their earlier education, need a clear sequence of instruction. *From Narrative Onward,* therefore, starts with a solid grounding in the development of a paragraph. Once students master the process involved in writing a paragraph, they have a basis for constructing body paragraphs and can readily make a transition to the more complex issues involved in essay writing. Similarly, language skills are ordered developmentally so that students build their understanding chapter by chapter.

That students learn about language most readily when vocabulary development and grammar are related to their own writing experience is our third assumption. To build this relationship, language skills are integrated into the work of the chapter. Examples from the professional writing serve as starting points for vocabulary and usage instruction. Exercises challenge students to write their own examples, and the revision section of each chapter asks students to apply what they are learning to their own paragraphs and essays.

Over the last several years, students in our more than a dozen writing classes have developed competency in written communication skills using the text material. The text has adapted to individual, small group, and full class needs in sections that meet mornings, afternoons, or evenings. In these classes, we have observed students become interested in and excited about their work. *From Narrative Onward* has promoted fluency as students write about what they know and focus on thinking skills that lead to solid academic writing.

Features of This Text

From Narrative Onward offers the following features.

- **Writing by professional authors** Selections by professional writers provide students with models of good writing for analysis of content, technique, and theme. These selections offer a foundation for exploring themes of universal significance. Each chapter theme is the springboard for student writing based on personal experience.
- **Reading-writing connection** The elements of active learning—talking and listening, writing, reading, and reflecting—are emphasized in each chapter. Thoughtful questions related to the professional writing engage students in pre-reading, focused active reading, responsive writing, and paragraph and essay writing. In integrating reading with writing, students discover, process, and apply information.
- **Process-oriented writing** Since writing is a complex, recursive, dynamic process, each chapter focuses on four stages of writing: prewriting, organizing ideas, writing, and rewriting. In this process-oriented approach, the initial focus is on content, not the mechanics of writing. Diagrams and models of prewriting, organizing ideas, and writing illustrate instruction.
- **Focus on pre-writing techniques** To encourage students to try a variety of pre-writing techniques and to learn which ones they prefer, the text introduces, explains, and models a procedure for brainstorming and gathering ideas in each chapter. By focusing on one technique at a time, students gain a wide repertoire of experience, including journal keeping, focused free writing, listing, questioning, clustering, looping, visualizing, recording sensory details, making a comparison chart, and interviewing.
- **Sequenced instruction** Each chapter strand progresses sequentially in increasing difficulty. Pre-writing techniques begin with simple journal writing and end with the more sophisticated technique involving interviewing. Grammar skills start with subject, verb, and phrase identification and proceed to simple, compound, and complex sentences. As importantly, writing assignments advance from a basic narrative paragraph to a persuasive essay.
- **Language skills in context** Form and mechanics are meaningful when they are taught in the context of actual writing. For that reason, language skills are pre-

sented in context of the chapter theme. Chapter exercises involve working with vocabulary denotation and connotation, as well as concepts of grammar and mechanics using words, sentences, and paragraphs from the reading selections.

- **Sentence rearrangement and sentence combining** Using sentences based on the reading selection, students practice rearranging sentences to change sentence emphasis and combining sentences to increase fluency of style. With its emphasis on writing more sophisticated sentence structures, sentence rearrangement and combining is an effective way for students to understand the principles of grammar.
- **Application-based activities** Application-based activities emphasize active learning. Sentence rearrangement and sentence combining exercises require students to reconstruct sentences by changing the sentence's "surface" while retaining the sentence's meaning. Vocabulary exercises involve considering multiple meanings and explaining how subtle differences in synonyms affect meaning. Grammar exercises require students to write their own sentence illustrations. Each chapter concludes with revision exercises so that students apply the language skills developed throughout the text to their own composition.
- **Grammar supplement** An overview of grammar, usage, and mechanics provides a ready reference. Illustrating each concept is a thought-provoking quotation. Exercises reinforce understanding of and proficiency in using language.

We would like to acknowledge the numerous students from our classes at Monroe Community College who reinforced our efforts as we developed *From Narrative Onward.* A special thanks goes to our students Evelyn Garcia, Peter Pacilio, and Sandor Baldor. In addition, we offer our appreciation to Judi Salsburg, Ellen Baker, and Matthew Fox in the Transitional Studies Department at Monroe Community College for offering their suggestions to the Instructor's Manual.

Second, we thank the many reviewers who offered suggestions:

Rabe Harris, Houston Community College (Texas), Florida Memorial College

Karen H. Soutar, Aims Community College (Colorado)

Janet R. Goldstein, Bramson ORT Technical Institute (New York)

Virginia "Jinna" F. Clark, Gordon College, University System of Georgia

Kathleen Rice, Ivy Tech State College (Indiana)

Third, our sincere gratitude is extended to the staff at Houghton Mifflin Company, including Mary Jo Southern, Jennifer Roderick, Kellie Cardone, Fred Burns, and Liz Napolitano, who helped bring this textbook to fruition, and to Suzanne Hinderliter, with whom we first discussed writing a textbook for our students.

Finally, special tribute must to go our respective families for their helpful suggestions and unwavering support and encouragement. To John, who unselfishly and tirelessly helped us unravel the complexities of our computers and software, and who cooked us many dinners, so we could devote more time to writing our textbooks, we give our heartfelt thanks.

Diane Fitton
Barbara Warner

From Narrative Onward
Writing With Focus

PART ONE

Paragraph Writing

CHAPTER 1

Memories

Memories: Exploring the Theme

The Lost Garden by Laurence Yep

Focusing on Paragraph Structure

Topic Sentence
Supporting Sentences
Concluding Sentence
Title

Developing a Paragraph

Assignment 1: Writing about Memories
The Writing Process
Work on Writing Assignment 1

Building Language Skills

Vocabulary
Subjects and Prepositional Phrases
Sentence Style

Revising the Paragraph

Memories: Exploring the Theme

A selection by a professional author introduces each unit in this text. The reading focuses on a theme that is important to people no matter who they are, where they live, what their age or background, or what their experiences. If you are human, you are affected in some way by these themes.

This first chapter explores the concept of memory. The countless memories that people collect over the years can be a rich source for writing. Reading about someone else's memories may help you remember some of your own experiences and consider how they are similar to or quite different from the author's. You may also be reminded of memories that you would like to share.

As you read this selection about memory, become aware of how you read. Reading is more than moving your eyes across the words on a page, just as watching a movie is more than staring at a screen. Whether you realize it or not, when you are watching a movie, you are making connections between what is happening on the screen and what you already know about a topic. You are thinking about what is going on as the action happens, and you might even be thinking ahead to what might happen.

In the same way, when you are reading, you need to be involved. That means you start by making connections with what you already know about the topic, you react as you read, you predict what will come next, and you think about what the author has said when you finish the reading.

As you prepare to read, answering some questions can help you get involved with the topic.

EXERCISE 1 Prepare to Read

1. What kinds of things are people likely to remember?

____

____

____

2. What is the "garden of memories" that older people sometimes discuss? Why do they use the term "garden"?

____

____

____

3. Why do you suppose Laurence Yep called his writing "The Lost Garden"?

____

____

____

The Lost Garden by Laurence Yep

ABOUT THE AUTHOR

Growing up in San Francisco in the 1950s, Chinese-American Laurence Yep often felt alone and confused about his identity. As he wrote about his childhood memories, he became comfortable with his Chinese heritage. With the encouragement of an English teacher, he became a professional writer at age eighteen when he was paid a penny a word for his work. He says, "My Chinese-American books are a way of stepping into the shoes of members of my family."

---

1 Memories are like seeds. They lie concealed within the imagination—or perhaps they are buried even deeper, ripening with the quickening of the heart and growing according to the soul's own season. Planted in childhood, they sometimes do not bear fruit until long into adulthood. However, even if they lie sleeping within the imagination, within the heart, within the soul, they do not perish.[1]

2 Back in 1951, during Uncle Francis's wanderings, he and his wife, my Auntie Rachel, and their family wound up in Bridgeport, West Virginia. My mother's family had lived there for a time prior to their departure to California. Since my mother and Auntie Rachel had left Bridgeport as children, neither could remember the address of their old home; and yet once she was in that town, Auntie Rachel was able to trace her way back to the house.

3 Climbing the steps to the porch, my aunt knocked at the front door. When it was opened, she introduced herself to the present occupants of her old house. She chatted with them for a bit before they asked her if she would explain something that had been puzzling them for over twenty years. Taking her into the backyard, they showed her a particularly tenacious weed that they had been trying to get rid of for decades. They had chopped it with hoes, dosed it with herbicide,[2] and dug up its roots with

[1] **perish** die

[2] **herbicide** weed killer

spades. However, the plant kept growing back as if it were determined to stay.

4 It turned out to be a Chinese vegetable that my grandparents had planted so long ago. It had transplanted well from China to America, exasperating a generation of gardeners.

5 It may be something as simple and yet as indestructible as a weed that links us to our past and binds us to our dreams. Seeds, cast into strange soil, may thrive and grow—just like children and just like their memories. Memory never quite goes away. It is there, only hidden, like the laughter of unseen children in a garden. A home can be cemented over but never buried. Adults can put up steel and lay asphalt, but their buildings and streets can never outlast memory. Memory pays no rent and is assessed no taxes, yet its value is infinite.[3]

Reading includes taking time to understand and react to what you have read. Writing about what you read is one of the best ways to gain understanding because it requires you to think through and organize new ideas. You are actively engaged in discovering what the author means and then reacting to these ideas by considering your own perspectives.

The questions that you are asked to answer are arranged in increasing order of complexity. At the first level, **Finding Facts,** you find answers to questions that your fellow readers, your classmates and your instructor, will agree with. No one will dispute the answer because everyone will find the same one in the reading.

Finding Facts Where did Yep's mother's family live before they moved to California?

Fact Found Bridgeport, West Virginia

At the second level, **Making Inferences,** you must go beyond finding facts to creating inferences by expressing your interpretation of what the reading means.

Making Inferences Why does Yep tell us about the "tenacious weed" that the residents of Auntie Rachel's old house tried so hard to kill?

Inference Made The "weed" that wouldn't die is a symbol of our memories. Just as the weed did not die despite the new residents' attempts to kill it, so too our memories stay with us even if we do not think about them for a long time and even if we try to forget them.

[3] **infinite** immeasurable, boundless

At the third level, **Sharing Reactions,** you consider how the author's views are like or unlike your own. You evaluate what the author has said in light of your own experience.

> **Sharing Reactions** Do you agree that memories are like seeds? Why or why not?
>
> **Reactions Shared** I think Yep has a point. Our memories are waiting to be tapped into or to be brought to life, just as a seed given sunlight and water can be made to grow or be brought to life. Sometimes, when I sit down and play the piano, I remember the times when I was a little girl visiting my grandparents' house and watching my grandmother joyfully playing the piano.

EXERCISE 2 Reflect on What You Have Read

Finding Facts

1. What was the origin of the weed that the occupants were trying to remove?

____

____

Making Inferences

2. Why does Yep mention the Chinese vegetable "transplanted well from China to America"?

____

____

____

____

Sharing Reactions

3. How does a person cultivate memories? In what ways is the cultivation of memories worthwhile?

____

____

FOCUSING ON Paragraph Structure

In each Chapter, you are introduced to an important concept about writing. As you apply these concepts to your own writing, you will produce increasingly more effective papers. In this Chapter, you learn about the structure of a basic component of writing, the paragraph.

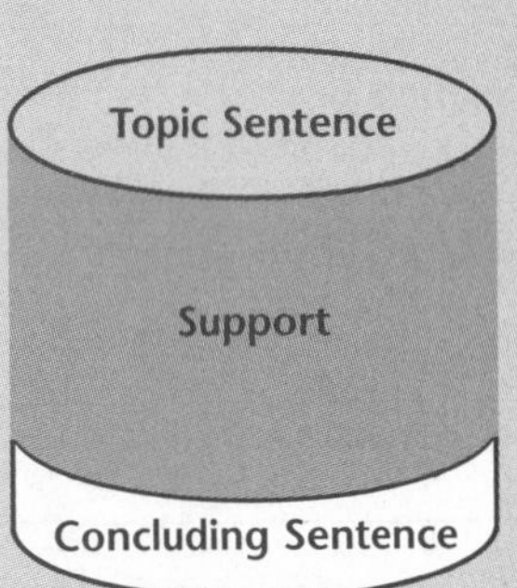

A group of sentences written together to develop a single idea is called a **paragraph.** A paragraph is an independent unit that can also function in a larger piece of writing, such as an **essay.**

A typical paragraph has a beginning that states its point, a middle that supports the point, and an end that concludes or completes the thought of the paragraph.

On average, a paragraph has eight to twelve sentences and 150–200 words. Depending on its topic and its purpose, however, a paragraph may be longer or shorter than average.

Topic Sentence

A paragraph focuses on one idea. This idea is stated in a sentence called the **topic sentence.** In most academic writing, the topic sentence is the first sentence of the paragraph. Think of the topic sentence as the statement of a contract the writer makes with the reader. The writer agrees to develop the stated idea in a way that is clear and complete. The contract is fulfilled when every sentence following the topic sentence relates to it.

A topic sentence has two parts: the topic to be discussed and the writer's reaction to the topic. The topic and the reaction must be limited in scope so that they can be developed in the single paragraph. With an effective topic sentence, you are well on your way to creating a successful paragraph.

What makes an effective topic sentence? Consider the following topic sentences:

Example 1

Weak topic sentences

I have memories of third grade.

This sentence is **weak.** Although there is a topic, "memories of third grade," there is **no reaction** to this topic.

I have **wonderful** memories of third grade.

This sentence is stronger than the first because of the addition of the reaction word "wonderful," but the idea is probably **too broad** to develop in a single paragraph.

Effective topic sentences

I have wonderful memories of **my third grade teacher.**

I have wonderful memories of my third grade teacher **reading *The Indian in the Cupboard* to the class.**

Adding specific information improves the topic sentence by limiting the discussion and including a reaction.

Example 2

Weak topic sentence

I went to many schools because of my father's job.

This sentence is weak because it is not specific about "my father's job," and there is no reaction to the topic.

Effective topic sentence

I had **a hard time keeping up** in school because my father's job **meant we moved a lot.**

This topic sentence is a good one since it clarifies the topic and gives the writer's reaction.

Example 3

Weak topic sentence

In eighth grade I had an attitude.

The topic is too broad to be developed in one paragraph.

Effective topic sentence

In eighth grade my attitude about school caught up with me.

This topic sentence is appropriately limited to the writer's attitude about eighth grade and includes a reaction that actions have a consequence.

Supporting Sentences

The main idea of a paragraph, expressed in the topic sentence, can be developed with examples, details, reasons, definitions, and comparisons. Notice how the supporting sentences that follow explain how the author's attitude about school caught up with him.

Example

Topic sentence

In eighth grade my attitude about school caught up with me.

Supporting sentences

Although I was generally a smart kid, I thought the only way I could fit in was to get kicked out of class and show that I was a tough guy. My trouble was mainly in science class. I was so annoying and bad that everyday as I walked into class, my teacher, Mr. Joss, had a referral written out for me. In my other classes, my teachers tried talking to me, but I thought I knew better. Because of my attitude, I failed almost every test. One day at the end of the year, my father, the school counselor, and the eighth grade principal met to discuss whether I should proceed to the ninth grade. They, not I, were discussing it. I was just present.

Concluding Sentence

The concluding sentence is the final sentence of the paragraph. The purpose of this sentence is to remind the reader of the topic sentence and provide a brief reference to the content of the paragraph. The concluding sentence indicates that the point of the paragraph has been made and the paragraph is finished.

Example 1

To this day, I enjoy listening to a good story read out loud.

Example 2

Hard as it was, I think changing schools was all for the good.

Example 3

It was decided that I would spend yet another year in the eighth grade.

Title

The title of the paragraph is written at the top of the paper. Similar to the title of a movie or book, the title should be a few words that entice someone to become involved. While fairly representing the contents, the title of a paragraph can be a question, a clever twist of words, or simply a straightforward word or phrase. Capitalize the first, the last, and all important words in the title.

Example 1

A Third Grade Story

Example 2

Neither Here nor There

Example 3

Eighth Grade Again

Developing a Paragraph

From your life experiences, you have abundant information for writing. It's all there—who you are, where you have been, what has happened to you, what interests you, how you see others, and why you believe as you do. In the writing assignment for each unit, you are asked to use information drawn from yourself to respond to the theme of the chapter.

Assignment 1: Writing about Memories

Laurence Yep writes about a vegetable plant brought from China years before. This plant continues to flourish in the garden despite efforts to get rid of it. For Yep, this plant brings back memories of his life in a Chinese-American family. Similarly, most people have a vast store of memories, sometimes deeply rooted, that with appropriate nurturing grow clear in the imagination.

Begin to nurture some of your memories. Think especially about what you remember from your school days. Can you picture your elementary school building? Your high school? A classroom? The cafeteria? The gym? The school grounds? Who were your teachers? Coaches? Who were your classmates? Specifically, what experiences do you remember? You will probably remember some major events, such as sixth-grade graduation or the junior prom. You will also remember happenings that were important to you alone—the day you met the person who became a good friend, the moment you learned you had been cut from the basketball team, or the time you passed your math test. You may remember times when you felt strong emotion. When were you happy, embarrassed, sad, angry, courageous, curious, or frightened? Answering these and other questions you think of will help you connect with memories, both positive and negative, of events from your school days.

For Writing Assignment 1, write a paragraph that tells about a school memory.

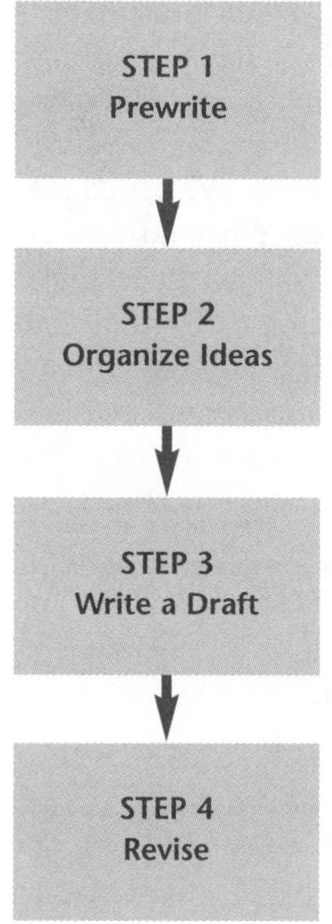

STEP 1 Prewrite Before you begin to write a paper, you want to make sure you understand the writing assignment. Then, you should spend time gathering ideas by writing what you know about the topic. You will practice using different prewriting techniques for each unit.

STEP 2 Organize Ideas After you gather your ideas about a topic, decide on the main idea of your paper. You then organize the supporting details in a logical order.

STEP 3 Write a Draft During this part of the process, you use the ideas you have organized to write a draft of your composition.

STEP 4 Revise Revising means reworking your rough draft so that in your final draft your ideas are clear, well ordered, and convincing.

The Writing Process

You can compare prewriting with getting ready to do some physical activity. When you work out or take part in a sports activity, how do you begin? You most likely get your body ready by warming up and stretching. Just as there are many ways to stretch your body, there are a variety of ways to prewrite or warm-up for writing.

Journal Keeping

Prewriting Technique

Many professional writers keep diaries or journals. These informal, personal notes provide a record of events, thoughts, feelings, and other information that can be a springboard to more formal writing. When you write in a journal, you focus on writing down your reactions. You are not concerned about complete sentences, beginnings and endings, spelling, or punctuation marks. To make a journal meaningful, you want to react to the events of your life, both ordinary and exceptional. Why is eating breakfast important to you? What do you notice about other drivers as you navigate the expressway? Use your journal to get comfortable with writing; explore ideas and play with words. When you keep a journal, your entries become an *idea bank* for you to reread, think about, and use for writing assignments.

Read an example of a journal entry that explores different school memories.

School memories. Yeah. Right. How do I pinpoint something memorable when all I remember is moving from school to school? Let's see—how many schools did I attend? Ten? Should I count the school I went to for one day? The principal made me get my books, go to first period, even though I told her we were moving to Tennessee that afternoon. She didn't believe me until my dad came to pick me up. All those years. I can remember either being bored out of my mind because the next school was covering something I already learned in the last school or having a sense of panic that I didn't know what was going on. If nothing else, I suppose the experience taught me flexibility, to take advantage of the moment. In Massachusetts the kids called me Johnny Reb. I was a short scrawny kid with a southern accent. I'll never forget Connecticut. I was the new kid in the freshman class, and two upper-classmen had it in for me. For months they were after me. Then, one Friday evening, after a football game they came after me. I lunged for the bigger kid, kicking and flailing with all my might. They left me alone after that.

I stayed the longest in Texas. A year. Fifth grade. I'll never forget how my kid sister got me mixed up with the school bully. What a mean bastard he was. Tex. Picked fights for no reason and he always won. Didn't care if he was sent to the principal's office. His two sisters were nice, but he argued with everybody. He started to pick on Jan—she never knew how to keep quiet. In the end it all worked out. I even felt I won the day. I got so mad and Tex and I started pushing each other around. He backed down. Yeah, I remember it all clearly now. Tex had to do something to save face. He challenged me to a bike race. We both had brand-new bikes we got for our birthdays. I remember I was so excited that day. I just had to accept the challenge. We raced around the parking lot, and the one who got around those cement things three times was winner. It was neck and neck. Then Tex shoved me into the cement, into the curb. Flipped over the handlebars. Now that's a story worth writing about.

A Paragraph Plan

Before writing the paragraph, you will find it helpful to outline or map out a plan for ordering the ideas you will present. This plan can be simply a sketch, or it can be a formal outline, whichever is appropriate for you and the subject matter. You may use it as it is, or you may need to revise it as you write. Here is the informal outline the writer made from his journal entry.

Title **Tex Backed Down**

Topic Sentence

One of my proudest memories is standing up to the grade school bully.

What happened at the beginning of the event?

Tex teased my sister Jan.

I stood up for my sister.

Tex backed down when we started pushing each other around.

Then what happened?

Tex challenged me to a bike race.

The race was close.

Tex shoved me into the cement.

My bike was ruined.

What happened at the end?

I amazed my friends, and I felt great.

A Model Paragraph

When you have ideas and a plan, you are ready to write a draft. This **first draft,** also called a **rough draft,** is a first try at getting ideas together. The draft usually needs additional work to make it ready for readers. Most authors need to write several drafts before they are satisfied with their work.

After writing several drafts, here is the writer's final copy.

TEX BACKED DOWN

One of my proudest memories is standing up to the grade school bully. One day when my sister Jan was about seven and I was ten, we ran into the school tough guy, Tex, in the schoolyard. Tex was known as the tough guy because he would fight anybody at any time and win, and he just had a bad attitude. For some reason, my little sister started talking back to Tex, and I, trying to protect her, ended up in a scuffle with him. Amazingly enough, after I pushed him hard a few times, Tex backed down. To this day, I don't know why he backed down, but he did. Tex had to do something to save face so he challenged me to a bike race. I accepted the challenge. I figured I had already won when Tex backed down, so losing a race would not matter at all. We raced around the school parking lot. Coming around the second lap, Tex cut me off and forced me into a cement island at the corner of the lot. After hitting the curb and crashing into a bush, I got up, picked up my bike, and rode away, a happy man. My friends wondered why I wasn't upset that Tex had made me crash or that Jan had caused a fight. "Who cares," I said. "Tex backed down from me."

Work on Writing Assignment 1

This section provides an opportunity for you to go through the steps of the writing process.

EXERCISE 3 Prewrite, Plan, and Draft

Part A

Write a journal entry about the topic "A School Memory." Reread your entry. Continue writing to respond to these questions: What was your reaction to the event when it happened? What is your reaction to the memory now?

Part B

Using ideas from your journal entry and other ideas you think of, write a plan for your paragraph.

Title ______________________________

Topic sentence ______________________________

What happened at the beginning of the event you remember? ______________________________

____

Then what happened? ______________________________

____

____

What happened at the end? What is your concluding thought?

____

Part C

Use your plan to write a draft of your paper.

Building Language Skills

In each unit, before you prepare a final draft of your paper, you are provided with some important skills to apply to your writing. With practice, you will find your writing becoming increasingly clear and convincing.

Vocabulary

Why is building vocabulary important for competent writing? The more you know about words, the more able you are to choose those that make your point. The most appropriate word is not the longest word you know, but simply the word that says most precisely what you mean.

A valuable guide to words is a collegiate dictionary—a standard hard-covered edition for your study location and a paperback edition for class. You are probably familiar with a **dictionary;** it provides definitions, pronunciations, various spellings, and histories of thousands of words.

Another useful guide to words is a **thesaurus,** which supplies lists of synonyms (similar words) and antonyms (opposite words). To distinguish among synonyms and antonyms when you do not know their meanings, use a dictionary. The dictionary and thesaurus features on a word-processing program can be helpful in editing your papers. Each chapter in this text encourages you to develop vocabulary skills.

Word Meanings

As you know, a word may have more than one meaning. Being aware of multiple meanings is important in using a word correctly.

For example, what is the meaning of the word **tenacious**?

The dictionary definitions of "tenacious" include

1. holding fast
2. stubborn, persistent
3. able to remember
4. not easily pulled apart
5. sticky

What dictionary definition is used in the following sentence?

"Taking her into the backyard, they showed her a particularly **tenacious** weed that they had been trying to get rid of for decades."

The second definition, "stubborn or persistent," is the closest definition since the weed grows back year after year.

EXERCISE 4 Use the Dictionary

Use a dictionary to find the meanings of the word **cast.**

Dictionary meanings

____

____

____

____

____

____

____

____

Underline the dictionary definition of the word as it is used in the following sentence:

"Seeds ***cast*** into strange soil, may thrive and grow."

Synonyms

Synonyms are words that have similar, but not exactly the same, meanings. Paying attention to the subtleties of meaning will help you to choose words with precision. What happens to the meaning of the sentence when a synonym such as **pounded, rapped,** or **tapped** is substituted for the word **knocked** in the following sentence?

"Climbing the steps to the porch, my aunt **knocked** at the front door."

Knocking at the door is a polite action. If the aunt **pounded,** she would be assertive or aggressive. **Rapping** shows an insistence to be heard. If the aunt **tapped,** she could be showing a concern about disturbing the occupants.

EXERCISE 5 Use the Thesaurus

Explain how the meaning of the phrase is altered by each synonym.

1. **climbing** up the steps to the porch ______________________________

   ____

2. **scrambling** up the steps to the porch ______________________________

   ____

3. **crawling** up the steps to the porch ______________________________

   ____

4. **bounding** up the steps to the porch ______________________________

   ____

By studying how the English language is structured, you can see how sentences are put together and can create grammatically correct sentences of your own.

Subjects and Prepositional Phrases

Learning about the parts of the sentence gives you a vocabulary for discussing your sentences. It is important, for example, to know that every English sentence has a **subject.**

What is a Subject?

The subject of a sentence tells **"who"** or **"what"** the sentence is about.

Look at the following sentences:

> Memories are like seeds.

The subject of this sentence tells **"what"** the sentence is about: ***memories***

> Back in 1951, my uncle and his wife, my Auntie Rachel, wound up in Bridgeport, West Virginia.

The subject of this sentence tells **"who"** the sentence is about: ***my uncle and his wife, my Auntie Rachel.***

The most common place to find the subject is at the beginning of a sentence. Right away, the writer is telling you **"who"** or **"what"** the sentence is going to be about.

Auntie Rachel was able to trace her way back to the house.

Auntie Rachel is **"who"** the sentence is about.

They had chopped the weed with hoes, dosed it with herbicide, and dug up its roots with spades.

They (referring to the new residents) is **"who"** the sentence is about.

Memory never quite goes away.

Memory is **"what"** the sentence is about.

My mother and Auntie Rachel left Bridgeport as children.

The *old home* and the *Chinese plant* brought back memories to Auntie Rachel.

To find the subject of a sentence that is a question, turn the question into a statement and then find the subject.

Question: Why did Auntie Rachel trace her way back to the house?

Question turned into a statement: Auntie Rachel did trace her way back to the house.

The subject is *Auntie Rachel.*

Or, the question word itself can be the subject.

What never goes away?

The subject of the sentence is *what.*

Without a subject, a sentence is incomplete. Because the sentence is the basic unit used to express an idea, writing with incomplete sentences can cause a problem for the reader. The reader expects that each group of words written as a sentence will state a complete idea. When a subject is missing, the group of words is incomplete, and the reader can become confused, misunderstanding the writer's meaning.

EXERCISE 6 Supply a Subject

Complete each sentence by supplying a subject that makes sense. Use a different word or words for each sentence.

1. Taking her into the backyard, ____________________ showed her a weed.
2. Planted in the garden are ____________________.
3. For a time ____________________ lived there.
4. ____________________ was able to trace her way back.
5. Through the years ____________________ kept growing back.
6. ____________________ pays no rent?
7. ____________________ were in town.
8. ____________________ was interesting.
9. Fortunately, ____________________ found the place.
10. ________ and ________ could not remember the address of their old home.

What is a Prepositional Phrase?

To locate subjects, you will find that knowing about prepositional phrases is helpful. Prepositions are words that introduce prepositional phrases. The subject is **never** in a prepositional phrase. Learn to recognize the following commonly used prepositions:

Direction	Position	Time	Other
along	above	after	by
into	across	at	with
down	against	before	without
over	among	by	against
through	around	during	except
to	at	in	for
toward	before	since	of
up	behind	until	like
from	beneath	within	
	beside		
	between		
	by		
	in		
	off		
	on		
	under		
	upon		
	within		

A **preposition** is always the **first** word of a group of related words. The preposition combined with its group of related words is called a **prepositional phrase.** Prepositional phrases add information to a sentence and may describe position *(in that town),* direction *(from China),* or time *(during Uncle Francis' wanderings);* or they may show some other relationship *(of her old house).*

1. When you are studying the structure of a sentence, it is a good idea to locate the prepositional phrases first and then look for the subject among the words that are not in a prepositional phrase.

   Memory is ~~like the laughter of unseen children in a garden~~.

   With the prepositional phrases located, it is clear that the subject of the sentence is **memory.**

2. A prepositional phrase can be placed anywhere in the sentence where it makes sense.

   The plant kept growing back.

   Prepositional phrase: ***in the garden***

At the beginning of the sentence:	**In the garden** the plant kept growing.
In the middle of the sentence:	The plant **in the garden** kept growing.
At the end of the sentence:	The plant kept growing **in the garden.**

EXERCISE 7 Add a Prepositional Phrase

Referring to the list of prepositions, add a prepositional phrase to each sentence. Indicate how the prepositional phrase adds to or changes the meaning of the sentence.

EXAMPLE

The seeds are buried.

The seeds are buried *in the spring.*

Adding *in the spring* clarifies when the event happened.

1. The plant kept growing.______________________________________

   ____

2. The door was opened. ______________________________

____

3. Memories lie sleeping. ______________________________

____

4. My mother's family lived there. ______________________________

____

5. They chatted.______________________________

____

6. The weed is there.______________________________

____

7. She introduced herself.______________________________

____

8. They dug up its roots.______________________________

____

9. The family moved.______________________________

____

Sentence Style

In this section, you gain flexibility in writing sentences. This skill is important in structuring sentences that clearly convey your meaning. The ability to vary word order and combine sentences also gives you techniques to develop sentences that flow smoothly and connect seamlessly one to the next.

Sentence Rearrangement

The ability to use a variety of sentence patterns adds interest and reinforces the meaning of a sentence. See how the following sentence can be rearranged in several ways. Notice how the position of the subject moves as the order of the words changes.

> Planted in childhood, memories sometimes do not bear fruit until long into adulthood.
>
> **Rearranged:**
>
> Sometimes **memories** that were planted in childhood do not bear fruit until long into adulthood.
>
> In this rearranged sentence, writing the word "sometimes" first, in the most prominent position, emphasizes that the bearing of fruit in adulthood sometimes but not always happens.
>
> or
>
> **Memories** planted in childhood sometimes do not bear fruit until long into adulthood.
>
> In this rearranged sentence, writing "memories" as the first word puts the focus on the subject of the sentence, memories.
>
> or
>
> Long into adulthood, the **memories** that were planted in childhood sometimes bear fruit.
>
> In this rearranged sentence, the focus shifts to the prepositional phrase written first. The emphasis is that the bearing fruit will happen "long into adulthood" when a person is older.

Which of the three rearrangements should the writer use? The answer first depends on what part of the sentence the writer wants to emphasize. Words placed at the beginning of a sentence receive the most emphasis. You as the writer can focus on what ideas are most important by thoughtfully arranging words in your sentence. Another consideration is the rhythm of the words as they are read. Try reading a sentence out loud with sentences that come before and after it to determine the most effective arrangement of words.

Following is a summary of how sentence parts can be rearranged to change the beginning of the sentence.

SENTENCE EMPHASIS

Emphasis	Example	
Who	whom the sentence is about	**The principal, my father, and I** sat in a small office on a cold, dreary winter day in order to discuss my future at Midwood High School.
Time	when something occurs	**On a cold, dreary winter day,** the principal, my father, and I sat in a small office in order to discuss my future at Midwood High School.
Place	where something is located	**In a small office** on a cold, dreary winter day, the principal, my father, and I sat in order to discuss my future at Midwood High School.
Manner	how or in what way something is done	**Sitting** in a small office on a cold, dreary winter day, the principal, my father, and I discussed my future at Midwood High School.
Cause	showing either the reason for something or the effect of something	**In order to discuss** my future at Midwood High School, the principal, my father, and I sat in a small office on a cold, dreary winter day.
Condition	under what circumstances something happens	**When** the principal, my father and I sat in a small office on a cold, dreary winter day, we discussed my future at Midwood High School.

EXERCISE 8 Rearrange Sentences

Rewrite each sentence using the indicated new beginning. Be sure to keep the meaning of the original sentence. Consider the effect of rearranging the words.

1. Memories lie concealed within the imagination.

   Within the imagination ______________________________

   ____

   ____

2. My mother's family lived for a time in the neighboring town of Bridgeport.

   For a time ______________________________

   ____

   ____

3. An image of an old neighborhood may linger on in our memory.

   In our memory ______________________________

   ____

   ____

4. My aunt climbed the steps to the porch and knocked at the front door.

   After ______________________________

   ____

   ____

Sentence Combining

Another way to make your writing more effective is to combine ideas from several sentences into a single sentence. Note the effect of these three short sentences.

They had chopped it with hoes.

They had dosed it with herbicide.

They had dug up its roots with spades.

Here is one sentence combining the ideas:

They had chopped it with hoes, dosed it with herbicide, **and** dug up its roots with spades.

When the ideas are combined into one sentence, words can be eliminated. Putting the actions together connects the concepts.

Combining sentences makes your writing "tighter" and focuses meaning more clearly. The following groups of sentences are made more concise by combining them into one sentence.

1.

We found the house.

We lived in the house twenty years ago.

Combined: We found the house that we lived in twenty years ago.

2.

The plant was a vegetable.

It was from China.

It was sturdy.

My grandparents had transplanted it in America.

Combined: The sturdy plant was a vegetable from China that my grandparents had transplanted in America.

When you combine sentences, consider the relationship you want to establish among the ideas, and use a word to convey that relationship.

SENTENCE RELATIONSHIPS

Combine ideas to . . .	Examples
add another part of equal importance	and, or, moreover
point out a contrast	but, yet, however, although
indicate a conclusion or result	so, therefore, consequently, because, since
specify a condition	if, unless
show sequence	subsequently, then, while, when
add details	that, which, who, where

EXERCISE 9 Combine Sentences

Combine the ideas from the sentences in each group to write one new sentence. As you write each sentence, consider the emphasis and relationships you want to achieve.

EXAMPLE

Memories are planted in childhood.

Memories do not perish.

Memories that are planted in childhood do not perish.

1.

The new occupants chatted with my aunt.

They asked her to explain something.

___

___

___

2.

The plant was a Chinese vegetable.

The plant was indestructible.

___

___

___

3.

Buildings can never outlast memory.

Streets can never outlast memory.

___

___

___

Revising the Paragraph

Earlier in this chapter when you finished writing your draft, you may have been tempted to think, "Now, that's done!" Tell yourself, "Not so fast. I can make my paper better." Ideally, you will have time to put the first draft of your paper away for a bit and come back to it when you are fresh and ready to work. Then, you will begin an important part of your assignment—**revising.**

Revising literally means "seeing again." To revise, you will look at your draft with a critical eye to make sure you have written your ideas clearly and completely in logical order. This process involves rethinking and reworking your paper.

EXERCISE 10 Rework for Content, Structure, and Accuracy

Part A

Revise your paragraph by checking that it has a topic sentence and includes the information you need to make your memory clear. Reread the last sentence of your paragraph to be sure it provides a conclusion. Change words and sentences as necessary; you may even need to write a second draft. Finally, check to be sure that you have a title.

Part B

In your draft, locate the subjects of your sentences by placing brackets around each. If you cannot locate a subject, you may not have a sentence. Add a subject to any group of words without a subject, and rewrite each sentence so that the subject is clear.

Part C

Using the changes you made in your draft, write a final copy of your paragraph.

Proofread your paper to correct misspelled words, typographical errors, and missing words.

One technique for catching mistakes is to read your paper out loud. Often you will find words you missed or put in by mistake. Another technique is to read your composition backwards from the end to the beginning, checking each sentence as a separate unit. Finally, it may be helpful to move a piece of solid white or colored paper down your draft so that you can focus on one line at a time. You can produce nearly error-free papers by training yourself to be your own editor.

CHAPTER 2

Decisions

Decisions: Exploring the Theme

Lives change because of decisions that are made. People sometimes make an important decision for themselves; often, however, especially in the case of young people, others make the decision for them. Whoever is responsible, a decision may produce either positive or negative results. Sometimes these results become apparent only after time has passed.

EXERCISE 1 Prepare to Read

1. Who should make decisions about children's schooling?

   ____

   ____

2. Should children be required to speak English in American schools? Why or why not?

   ____

   ____

From *Hunger of Memory* by Richard Rodriguez

ABOUT THE AUTHOR

Richard Rodriguez is the son of working-class parents who emigrated from Mexico to Sacramento, California. Before he went to school, he and his family spoke Spanish in their home. Going to school exposed him for the first time to the sounds and meanings of American English. This selection from his autobiography, *Hunger of Memory,* tells of coming to terms with a decision to speak only English at home. In 1997 Rodriguez, writer and editor, received the George Foster Peabody Award for essays on American life written for the PBS Show *The News Hour*. The Peabody Award recognizes "outstanding achievement in broadcast and cable."

---

1 Without question, it would have pleased me to hear my teachers address me in Spanish when I entered the classroom. I would have felt much less afraid. I would have trusted them and responded with ease. But I would have delayed—for how long postponed?—having to learn the language of

public society. I would have evaded—and for how long could I have afforded to delay?—learning the great lesson of school, that I had a public identity. . . .

2 Three months. Five. Half a year passed. Unsmiling, ever watchful, my teachers noted my silence. They began to connect my behavior with the difficult progress my older sister and brother were making. Until one Saturday morning three nuns arrived at the house to talk to our parents. Stiffly, they sat on the blue living room sofa. From the doorway of another room, spying the visitors, I noted the incongruity[1]—the clash of two worlds, the faces and voices of school intruding upon the familiar setting of home. I overheard one voice gently wondering, "Do your children speak only Spanish at home, Mrs. Rodriguez?" While another voice added, "That Richard especially seems so timid and shy."

3 With great tact the visitors continued, "Is it possible for you and your husband to encourage your children to practice their English when they are home?" Of course, my parents complied.[2] What would they not do for their children's well being? In an instant, they agreed to give up the language (the sounds) that had revealed and accentuated our family's closeness. The moment after the visitors left, the change was observed. *"Ahora, speak to us en ingles,"* my father and mother united to tell us.

4 At first, it seemed a kind of game. After dinner each night, the family gathered to practice "our" English. (It was still then *ingles,* language foreign to us, so we felt drawn as strangers to it.) Laughing, we would try to define words we could not pronounce. We played with strange English sounds, often overanglicizing our pronunciations. And we filled the smiling gaps of our sentences with familiar Spanish sounds. But that was cheating, somebody shouted. Everyone laughed. In school, meanwhile, like my brother and sister, I was required to attend a daily tutoring session. I needed a full year of special attention. I also needed my teachers to keep my attention from straying in class by calling out, Rich-heard. Their English voices slowly pried loose my ties to my other name, its three notes, Ri-car-do.

5 At last, seven years old, I came to believe what had been technically true since my birth: I was an American citizen. I was increasingly confident of my own public identity. But the special feeling of closeness at home was diminished by then. Gone was the desperate, urgent, intense feeling of being at home; rare was the experience of feeling myself individualized by

[1] **incongruity** awkwardness, strangeness, absurdity

[2] **complied** obeyed, agreed to

family intimates. We remained a loving family, but one greatly changed. No longer so close; no longer bound tight by the pleasing and troubling knowledge of our public separateness. Neither my older brother nor sister rushed home after school anymore. Nor did I. When I arrived home, there would often be neighborhood kids in the house. Or the house would be empty of sounds.

6 The family's quiet was partly due to the fact that, as we children learned more and more English, we shared fewer and fewer words with our parents. Sentences needed to be spoken slowly when a child addressed his mother or father. (Often the parent wouldn't understand.) The child would need to repeat himself. (Still the parent misunderstood.) The young voice, frustrated, would end up saying, "Never mind"—the subject was closed. Dinners would be noisy with the clinking of knives and forks against dishes. My mother would smile softly between her remarks; my father at the other end of the table would chew and chew at his food, while he stared over the heads of his children.

7 I would have been happier about my public success had I not sometimes recalled what it had been like earlier, when my family had conveyed its intimacy through a set of conveniently private sounds. Sometimes in public, hearing a stranger, I'd hark back to my past. One day, a dark-faced old woman—her hand light on my shoulder—steadied herself against me as she boarded a bus. She murmured something I couldn't quite comprehend. Her Spanish voice came near, like the face of a never-before-seen relative in the instant before I was kissed. Her voice, like so many of the Spanish voices I'd hear in public, recalled the golden age of my youth. Hearing Spanish then, I continued to be a careful, if sad, listener to sounds. Hearing a Spanish-speaking family walking behind me, I turned to look. I smiled for an instant, before my glance found the Hispanic-looking faces of strangers in the crowd going by.

EXERCISE 2 Reflect on What You Have Read

Finding Facts

1. What two worlds clashed when the teachers visited the Rodriguez home?

____

Making Inferences

2. Why did Mr. Rodriguez stare over the heads of his children during dinner?

____

Sharing Reactions

3. Did the parents make the right decision for their family? Why or why not?

____

____

____

FOCUSING ON Paragraph Support

Achieving clear communication involves looking at your writing from the perspective of your audience or reader. When you consider what information your audience needs to know in order to understand your message, you can make thoughtful decisions about what details to include in your paragraph.

Audience

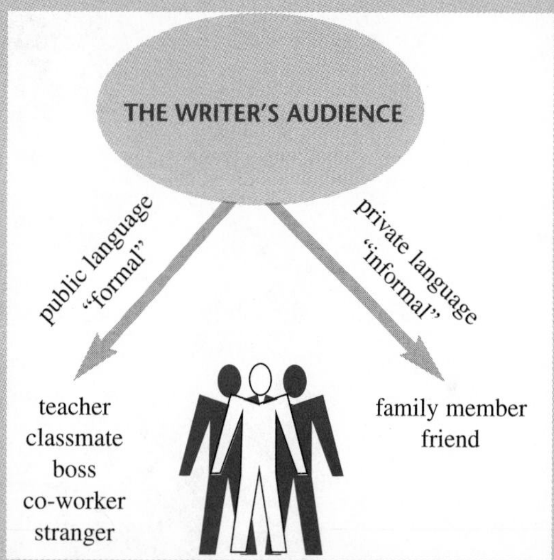

Your audience determines the overall approach of your presentation. When you write for family and friends, you can be casual. These people probably understand your message without much background information, and you may even have special words or slang for your communication.

On the other hand, when you are in a more formal situation with people who don't know you well, your language typically becomes more traditional, and your ideas may need more explanation.

People who don't know you at all depend on your using standard language and sufficient development so they are sure not to misinterpret your message. In school, you are usually writing for your class—your instructor and your peers—in an academic setting using Standard Written English.

Development

What is "just enough support"?

Just enough support is determined by your audience. Remember your readers have only the words you write to understand your meaning. Because they have not experienced with you what you are writing about, they cannot fill in gaps, cannot picture what you haven't described, and cannot understand what you haven't stated. To simplify your job of providing just enough of the right kind of information, envision different types of readers, each with a particular concern. There are the factual readers, the imaginative readers, the focused readers, and the curious readers. In reality, actual readers are varying combinations of any or all types so that when you write for each different type, you should be supporting your paragraph sufficiently.

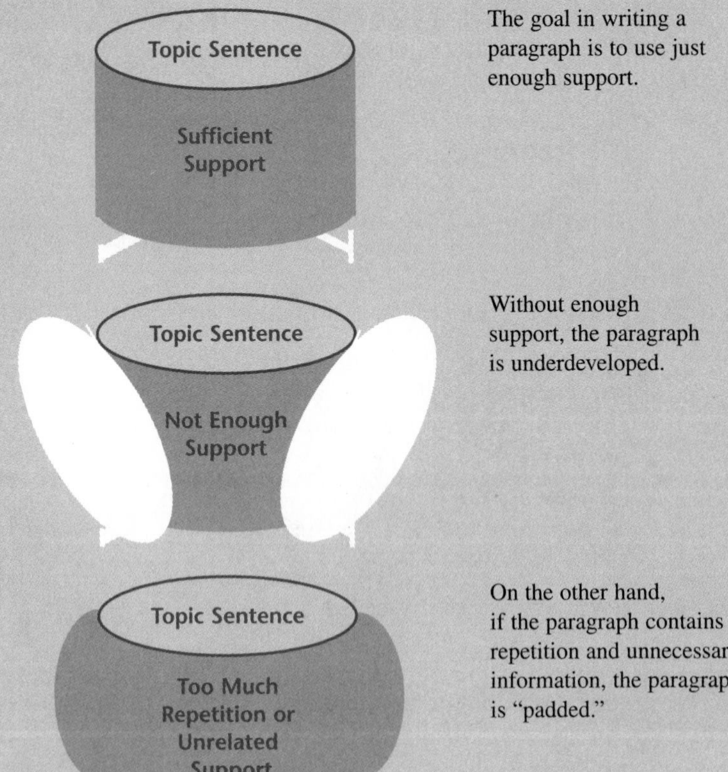

The goal in writing a paragraph is to use just enough support.

Without enough support, the paragraph is underdeveloped.

On the other hand, if the paragraph contains repetition and unnecessary information, the paragraph is "padded."

***FACTUAL READERS* want to know a lot of information about your topic.**

For **factual readers**, the **WRITER** must explain ideas clearly and logically. Ask yourself, "What kind of information would be helpful for readers who want to know specific details about this topic?"

Example

In order to provide more specific facts about the "kind of game" his family played to learn English, Rodriguez adds this information: "After dinner each night, the family gathered to practice our English. . . . We played with strange English sounds, often overanglicizing our pronunciations."

***IMAGINATIVE READERS* want to sense what you describe.**

For **imaginative readers**, the **WRITER** must describe by drawing pictures with words. Ask yourself, "What sights, sounds, smells, tastes, and textures can I describe to readers who have not experienced what I have?

Example

To help readers imagine how uncomfortable the parents must have felt when teachers visited their home, Rodriguez describes their awkwardness sitting on the sofa: "Stiffly, they sat on the blue living room sofa."

***FOCUSED READERS* like to focus on a main point; they lose interest reading something that is wordy, long-winded, or technical.**

For **focused readers**, the **WRITER** must be concise with explanations and detail. Ask yourself, "What sentences can be effectively combined? What is repetitious? What sentences drift from my topic sentence?"

***CURIOUS READERS* think of questions while reading.**

For **curious readers**, the **WRITER** anticipates questions and answers them. Be sure to answer questions curious readers might have about your topic. Ask yourself, "What else might the reader want to know?" Add these sentences.

Example

After the author writes, "We remained a loving family, but one greatly changed," he anticipates curious readers' questions by explaining why this change occurred. "The family's quiet was partly due to the fact that, as we children learned more and more English, we shared fewer and fewer words with our parents."

Developing a Paragraph

Assignment 2: Writing about Decisions

When Richard Rodriguez was in grade school, he was involved in a significant decision made by his parents. This decision was that the family would no longer speak Spanish at home.

Similarly, you may have been involved in a number of meaningful decisions. The decision may have been made for you. When you are young, for example, others decide where you will live; what schools you will attend; whether you will be involved with relatives, friends, and organizations. As you get older, you make more of your own decisions. Will you attend school? Where will you work? Will you remain in a relationship? Will you make a major purchase, such as a car or a house? Will you have children? In some cases, a family member, an employer, or someone else is in the position of decision making: Are you allowed to live at home? Will you keep your job?

A decision, no matter who makes it, is likely to have a "before." That is, there are reasons why a decision is made. In the selection for this chapter, the major reason for the decision not to speak Spanish at home was that the parents wanted their children to get a good education. In an effort to help the children, the parents supported the teachers, believing that speaking English at home would help Rodriguez and the other children become fluent in English.

A decision also has an "after"; that is, it has results. A result of the decision about speaking English at home for Rodriguez was that his home life was radically changed, leaving him emotionally adrift. Another, more positive result was that by speaking English at home, Rodriguez was better able to adjust to school life, and he learned to feel comfortable in public situations.

For Writing Assignment 2, write a paragraph that tells about a decision you or someone else made. Include either the reasons why the decision was made or the results of the decision.

The Writing Process

Focused Free Writing

Prewriting Technique

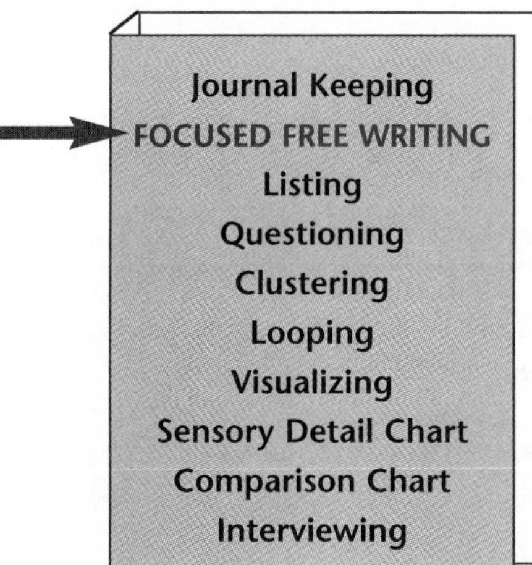

Free writing means simply writing on any topic and not worrying about beginnings and endings, spelling, punctuation, or grammar. **Focused free writing** or **directed writing** involves your writing nonstop on a given topic for several minutes. If you find your thoughts straying from the topic, you gently put yourself back on course. By writing nonstop, you discover what you know about the topic.

You may find yourself jumping from experience to experience as you explore the topic. This exploration can be useful. The important part about focused free writing is to keep writing so that you have a chance to explore a topic and write as much as possible. Then, reread your writing, underlining words that appeal to you because you like what they say or how they sound or because they remind you of more ideas. Gathering the useful ideas from your focused free writing will help you plan your paper. Following is an example of a student's focused free writing about decisions.

TOPIC: A DECISION THAT AFFECTED ME

What is a decision that affected me? I guess I could write about my parents getting divorced when I was a kid. That certainly affected me! No, I don't want to get into that. What else? I could write about the decision to repeat fourth grade. That was terrible. No friends, I cried and I hated my teacher and my mother for letting that happen. That's too depressing. Oh, I know, I remember when I was a senior I decided to buy a car. HA! It was rusted, and there was a tear in the back cushion, but it was mine and it gave me a way to get places. Now I remember, I got my first insurance bill and because I was 18 years old it cost a fortune. Mom said if I wanted my own car I had to be responsible for it, so I needed to get a job—fast. What a job! I decided to work in the injection mold shop in town. I always drove by it on the school bus, and I didn't give it much thought, but then I noticed a help wanted sign. I didn't really want to work there because it looked kind of run-down outside and there weren't many windows, but it wasn't far from home, so I wouldn't have to spend much money on gas. Now that I think of it, it was a good decision because I really learned to handle myself at a job. But it was a hard job. Those machines were huge and loud. At the end of the day, I wouldn't even put the car radio on because I needed it to be quiet for some time. I left that job when I went to college, but the funny thing is I can't look at a piece of plastic without knowing how good or bad it is.

A Paragraph Plan

A plan can be organized from the focused free writing.

Title Shop of Horrors

Topic Sentence My decision to take a job at an injection mold shop resulted in a frightful experience.

Beginning I was afraid of the machines.

Middle My job involved danger.
The factory was hot, smelly, and noisy.

End I had to fight "dinosaurs."

A Model Paragraph

Following is a paragraph based on the plan.

SHOP OF HORRORS

1 My decision to take a job at an injection mold shop resulted in a frightful experience. The shop was actually a factory where workers made various kinds of plastic parts. At first, I was afraid of the injection machines that looked like big and powerful creatures, standing 8 feet tall and 15 feet long. I had to put a mold inside the machine to form the plastic parts. Each time I did this, the safety gates across the opening of the mold would slam together loudly, making me jump backward. Then after the liquid plastic was injected into the mold and set, I had to remove the part. I was constantly fearful the powerful mold would crash together with my hand still in it. All the molded plastic that I removed was hot, so unless I was wearing a glove, the plastic pieces burned my hand. The acrid smell of the heated plastic stung my eyes, causing them to water all the time. All around me molds crashed together every few minutes. The thundering noise sounded as if dinosaurs were walking and shaking the earth. Little did I imagine when I decided to work at molding plastic that I would be fighting dinosaurs.

EXERCISE 3 React to the Paragraph

Answer the following questions to show your understanding of the use of support in the body of a paragraph.

1. What details does the writer provide for factual readers? ______

2. What details does the writer provide for imaginative readers? ______

3. Would focused readers want anything omitted? If so, what? ______

4. Would curious readers have questions? If so, what? ______

Work on Writing Assignment 2

EXERCISE 4 Prewrite, Plan, and Draft

Part A

Do focused free writing on decisions—their causes and their results. Underline ideas you can use for your paragraph.

Part B

From the ideas you underlined and other ideas you think of, organize a plan for your paper.

Part C

Use your plan to write a draft.

Building Language Skills

Vocabulary

EXERCISE 5 Use the Dictionary

Write dictionary definitions of the word *address*.

____

____

____

____

____

____

____

____

Underline the definition of the word as it is used in the following sentence:

> "Sentences needed to be spoken slowly when a child ***addressed*** his mother or father."

EXERCISE 6 Use the Thesaurus

Explain how the meaning of the phrase changes with the use of each synonym.

> "My mother would smile softly between her remarks; my father at the other end of the table would chew and chew at his food, while he ***stared*** over the heads of his children."

1. ***gazed*** over the heads of his children. ______________________________
2. ***watched*** over the heads of his children. ______________________________
3. ***gawked*** over the heads of his children. ______________________________
4. ***ogled*** over the heads of his children. ______________________________

Verbs

What is a verb?

Try reading groups of words from the reading selection *without* verbs.

> At first, it a kind of game. After dinner each night, the family to practice "our" English. Laughing, we to define words we not. We with strange English sounds, often overanglicizing our pronunciations. And we the smiling gaps of our sentences with familiar Spanish sounds.

Now read the words with the verbs added.

> At first, it ***seemed*** a kind of game. After dinner each night, the family ***gathered*** to practice "our" English. Laughing, we ***would try*** to define words we ***could*** not ***pronounce***. We ***played*** with strange English sounds, often overanglicizing our pronunciations. And we ***filled*** the smiling gaps of our sentences with familiar Spanish sounds.

Clue 1 If the word is a verb, it shows tense (time), either present, past, or future.

Past Tense	Present Tense	Future Tense
was (were) talking	am, is, are talking	will be talking
had talked	have talked	will have talked
had been talking	have (has) been talking	will have been talking

Clue 2 Some verbs show action, others express existence or being, and others link a subject with a word that means, identifies, or describes the subject.

Action Verbs

We ***played*** with strange English sounds, often overanglicizing our pronunciations.

We ***filled*** the smiling gaps of our sentences with familiar Spanish sounds.

Being Verbs

I ***was*** increasingly confident.

That ***is*** cheating.

The children ***were*** quiet.

Linking Verbs

At first, it ***seemed*** a kind of game.

We ***remained*** a loving family.

Clue 3 Some words are helping or auxiliary verbs because they help a main verb express a meaning that it could not express by itself.

List of Helping Verbs

is	were	has	may	might
am	do	have	can	could
are	did	had	shall	would
was	does	must	will	should

EXERCISE 7 Supply Verbs

Add a verb to complete each sentence.

EXAMPLE

For just an instant, I ___________

For just an instant, I remembered.

1. Smiling, ever watchful, my teachers ______________ my silence.
2. One Saturday morning, three nuns ________________ to talk to our parents.
3. She ___________ to me of my youth.
4. I ___________ sad.
5. Hearing a Spanish-speaking family walking behind me, I ______________.
6. We ________________ fewer and fewer words with our parents.

Clue 4 An infinitive is the base or root form of a verb with the word "to" before it. An infinitive is not used as a verb in a sentence.

Verb	Infinitive
lingered	to linger
heard	to hear
wrote	to write
was thinking	to think

EXERCISE 8 Supply Verbs

Complete each sentence by writing an appropriate verb form using the given infinitive.

EXAMPLE

Richard ___(to seem)___ so timid and shy.

Richard seems so timid and shy.

1. Stiffly, they ___(to sit)___ on the blue living room sofa.

2. From the doorway of another room, spying the visitors, I ___(to note)___ the incongruity.

3. I ___(to need)___ a full year of special attention.

4. Of course, my parents ___(to comply)___.

5. My parents ___(to agree)___ to give up our language.

Clue 5 Pay special attention to the infinitive "to be." The forms of "to be" are **am, is, are, was, were, being, been.** These verbs are the most commonly used in the English language.

EXAMPLES

It **was** still then *ingles,* language foreign to us.

But that **was** cheating.

Is it possible for you and your husband to encourage your children to practice their English when they **are** home?

EXERCISE 9 Use Forms of "To Be"

Write a form of the verb *to be* that makes sense in the sentence.

1. My mother _________ protective toward her family.

2. My brother and sister __________ in school.

3. Dinners __________ be noisy.

4. I _________ thinking about my past.

5. The Hispanic-looking faces of strangers in the crowd _________ going by.

Sentence Style

EXERCISE 10 Rearrange Sentences

Rewrite each sentence using the indicated new beginning. Be sure to keep the meaning of the original sentence. Consider the effect of rearranging the words.

1. After dinner each night, the family gathered to practice "our" English.

   The family gathered ______________________________

   ____

   ____

2. We remained a loving family, but one greatly changed.

   Although ______________________________

   ____

   ____

3. She murmured something I couldn't quite comprehend.

   I couldn't quite ______________________________

   ____

   ____

4. I smiled for an instant, and then I saw the Hispanic-looking faces of strangers in the crowd.

   Smiling ______________________________

   ____

   ____

EXERCISE 11 Combine Sentences

Combine the ideas from the sentences in each group to write one new sentence. As you write each sentence, consider the emphasis and relationships you want to achieve.

1.

I would have trusted them.

I would have responded with ease.

2.

We remained a loving family.

We were a greatly changed family.

3.

Dinners would be noisy.

The knives would clink against the dishes.

The forks would clink against the dishes.

4.

I arrived home.

There were neighborhood kids in the house.

____

____

____

Revising the Paragraph

EXERCISE 12 Rework for Content, Structure, and Accuracy

Part A

What information do you provide for factual readers? Imaginative readers? Curious readers? Revise your paragraph by adding these details.

Would focused readers want anything omitted? If so, omit these details.

Part B

Underline the subjects and verbs in each of your sentences. If you cannot find a subject and verb in a sentence, the sentence may be incomplete. Rewrite any group of words that does not have a subject and verb.

Part C

Using the changes you made in your draft, write a final copy of your paragraph.

Proofread your paper to correct misspelled words, typographical errors, and missing words.

CHAPTER 3

Identity

Identity: Exploring the Theme

How do you know when you are growing up? For many people, one sign of maturity is knowing yourself—understanding who you are, where you have come from, what you stand for, and where you are going. Coming to an understanding of yourself is not easy. It requires that you separate from and yet stay connected to your past. It means becoming a new person, while at the same time remaining part of the person you have been. The author of the reading in this chapter explains who he *is* by reflecting on who he *was*.

EXERCISE 1 Prepare to Read

1. How are older people important in a family or a community?

   ____

   ____

2. How can people separate from and yet stay connected to their past?

   ____

   ____

   ____

   ____

Notes of a Translator's Son by Joseph Bruchac

ABOUT THE AUTHOR

Joseph Bruchac, whose tribal affiliation is Abenaki, was born in 1942 in Saratoga Springs, New York. A storyteller and poet, he has published many books. An important theme for Bruchac, as a Native American writer, is finding a self-identity between two cultures. Carrying on the verbal tradition of his ancestors who told their stories orally, he shares his stories in writing. One of his stories was a PEN Syndicated Fiction Award Winner. A volume of interviews with Native American poets called *Survival This Way* was funded in part by a Rockefeller Foundation Humanities Fellowship. Bruchac's work has been translated into many languages.

1 Who am I? My name is Joseph Bruchac. The given name is that of a Christian saint—in the best Catholic tradition. The surname is from my father's people. It was shortened from *Bruchacek*—"big belly" in Slovak. Yet my identity has been affected by that small part of my blood which is American Indian and that comes to me from a grandfather who raised me.

2 I was a small child, often alone and often bullied. I was different—raised by old people who babied me, bookish, writing poetry in grade school, talking about animals as if they were people. My grandfather joked when he called me a "mongrel," a mixture of English and Slovak and "French," but others said such things without joking. When I was seven, I decided I would grow up to be so big and strong that no one would ever beat me up again. It took me nine years to do it. That winter of my junior year my grandmother died. My grandfather and I were left alone in the old house. That summer I grew six inches in height. In my senior year, though clothing and social graces showed little evolution, I became a championship wrestler, won a Regents' scholarship, and was accepted by Cornell University to study wildlife conservation.

3 How can I now, in only a few pages, cover the next twenty-five years? I can only go onward by going back to where my memories begin. The memory of me climbing the ladder, unafraid and right behind the old man, all the way to the roof forty feet up when I was only two, was my grandfather's. But it was recited about me so often that it became inseparably associated with my thoughts of my childhood. I still love high places, cliffs and trees, and resounding waterfalls. I inherited that fearlessness about high places and dying from my grandfather. I was always close to my grandfather. He delighted in telling how I was his shadow, how I carried my stick just like a spear and followed him everywhere. But, close as I was, he would never speak of the Indian blood that showed so strongly in him.

4 There are many people who could claim and learn from their Indian ancestry, but because of the fear their parents and grandparents knew, because of past and present prejudice against Indian people, that part of their heritage is clouded or denied. Had I been raised on other soil or by other people, my Indian ancestry might have been less important, less shaping. But I was not raised in Czechoslovakia or England. I was raised in the foothills of the Adirondack Mountains near a town whose spring waters were regarded as sacred and healing by the Iroquois and Abenaki alike.

5 I've avoided calling myself "Indian" most of my life, even when I have felt that identification most strongly, even when people have called me an "Indian." Unlike my grandfather, I have never seen that name as an insult,

6 but there is another term I like to use. I heard it first in Lakota, and it refers to a person of mixed blood, a *metis.* In English it becomes "Translator's Son." It is not an insult, like *half-breed.* It means that you are able to understand the language of both sides, to help them understand each other.

7 *The most widely anthologized of my poems describes one lesson I was taught in the way most good lessons come to you—when you least expect them. Let it represent that part of my life that has come from continual contact with Native American people over more than two decades.*

Birdfoot's Grampa

The old man
must have stopped our car
two dozen times to climb out and gather into his hands
the small toads blinded
by our lights and leaping, live drops of rain.
The rain was falling, a mist about his white hair and I kept saying you
    can't save them all accept it, get back in we've got places to go.
But, leathery hands full
of wet brown life
knee deep in the summer
roadside grass,
he just smiled and said
they have places to go to
too

EXERCISE 2 Reflect on What You Have Read

Finding Facts

1. What is the work of a "translator's son"? ______________________________

____

Making Inferences

2. What did the author learn from his grandfather?

____

____

____

Sharing Reactions

3. What does the author mean by saying, "I can only go onward by going back to where my memories begin"? Is this statement true for most people? Explain.

____

____

____

____

____

____

FOCUSING ON Order of Development

Organization

An important consideration is how to order the supporting points within your paragraph. You have a number of options.

Chronological order, also called **time order**, is the arrangement of details from beginning to end. When you use chronological order to write a paragraph, you arrange a series of events according to time: First, what happened? Then, what happened? Finally, what happened?

Order of importance, also called **emphatic order,** is the arrangement of details from least important to most important. When you use order of importance, you save the most important detail for the last point of the paragraph. In this way, you save the best for last, keeping your reader nodding in agreement through the end of your paragraph. Sometimes there is a reason for putting details in another order. Consider the point you want to make and order accordingly. The key is to invest some thought in the arrangement of your support.

Spatial order arranges details in a logical position or location. You use space order to describe an object, person, or location. You may want to order your details from top to bottom, side to side, front to back, or the other way around.

Outlining

An **outline** is a plan that organizes ideas to be presented in a paper. Like a blueprint a contractor uses to build a house, an outline is a plan that a writer uses "to build" or draft a paper. An outline includes the main idea and the supporting points in the order that they will be developed. Having an outline helps assure that a paper will be unified, logical, and complete.

A **paragraph outline** includes a topic sentence and a list of major points with supporting details listed in the order that they will be developed. The number of major points and supporting details will vary. An outline may be written as either sentences or phrases. By numbering each major point and lettering the supporting details, you have a graphic organization of your plan. It is not necessary to write the concluding sentence in an outline.

Topic Sentence

1. Major point
   a. Supporting detail
   b. Supporting detail
   c. Supporting detail
2. Major point
   a. Supporting detail
   b. Supporting detail
   c. Supporting detail
3. Major point
   a. Supporting detail
   b. Supporting detail
   c. Supporting detail

Developing a Paragraph

Assignment 3: Writing about Identity

Joseph Bruchac asks, "Who am I?" He concludes that he is a *metis,* a person who, because his heritage is both Euro-American and Native American, can help one group understand the other. Bruchac shows in his selection that he can answer his question "Who am I?" in a variety of other ways. He is a loving grandson, a climber with no fear of high places, a person unafraid of death, a former champion wrestler, a student of wildlife conservation. Bruchac is also a professional writer whose work has been translated into many languages.

"Who am I?" is a question considered by many reflective people. Like Bruchac, most people have many different answers to the question. Consider your answers to the question "Who are you?" Can you define yourself by a family relationship? *I am an appreciative son or a strict parent.* Your ethnic background or culture may be an important part of who you are. *I am a person proud of my Irish heritage. Celebrating holidays in the Cuban way is a part of who I am.* Maybe you can define yourself in terms of your work. *I am a skilled auto mechanic. I am responsible in my work as a sales associate.* Perhaps, a part of who you are is based on an interest or hobby. Are you an able gardener or a competent cook? Perhaps you are a traveler or an athlete, or you have a passion for movies.

For Writing Assignment 3, write a paragraph in which you answer the question, "Who am I?"

The Writing Process

Listing

Prewriting Technique

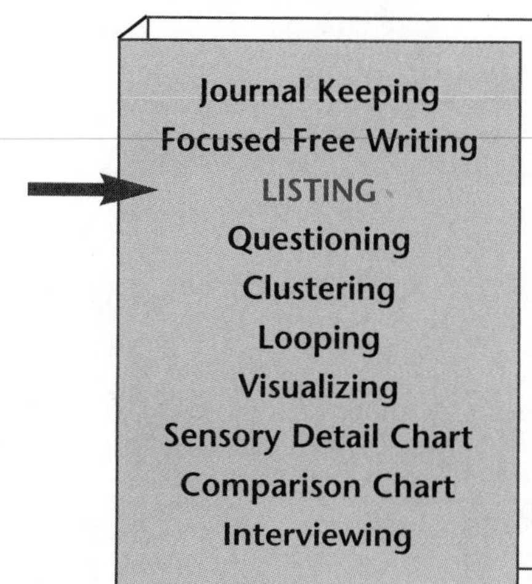

To gather ideas by listing or brainstorming, write a topic at the top of a sheet of paper and list whatever comes to mind. Don't stop to evaluate what you write. Just keep listing. Then reread your list, and try jotting down words that can be connected in some way next to the ones you wrote. In this way, you will have a large stock of ideas from which to draw. Circle the words that interest you and prompt more ideas.

Following is a list of words that relate to the question "Who Am I?" Words that can be connected are jotted down next to each one.

daughter	loved, protected, cared for
college student	degree, classes, studying
sister	youngest
musician	my passion, my future, instruments, lessons, composing
waitress	just for now
spiritual	daily prayers, weekly services
procrastinator	write papers night before
good friend	long conversations, companionship, support

A Paragraph Plan

Read how the writer organized her ideas.

Title Carolyn, I Am

Topic Sentence I am a musician in love with music.

1. Major point	1. early music
a. Supporting detail	a. Spinning Song
b. Supporting detail	b. captivating melody
2. Major point	2. instruments
a. Supporting detail	a. piano, percussion, guitar
b. Supporting detail	b. challenge
3. Major point	3. compositions
a. Supporting detail	a. past
b. Supporting detail	b. present

Analyze a Model Paragraph

Following is the paragraph written from the plan.

CAROLYN, I AM

I am a musician in love with music. My earliest memory of being completely in awe of music was as a five year old hearing my mother play "The Spinning Song" on the piano. Something in the melody captivated me. I remember dancing around the house to the tune lingering within me long after my mother had stopped playing. Since that time, I have learned to play the piano, percussion, and guitar. With each instrument, I enjoyed the initial challenges of trying to make a "pleasant" sound and then patiently learning to make "real" music. When I'm not playing an instrument or listening to music, I often hear "ideas" for new songs in my head. Melodies, rhythms, and sounds interconnect with my feelings to suggest a tune that I must compose. Today, when I listen to songs I composed years ago, I can recapture the feelings I had. At such moments, I don't feel like a twenty-two year old, but a teenager, one minute in love and the next, in agony. The silly, playful songs I now compose for children remind me of the joyful times of being so young. For me, music is not only what occupies my free time, it is a part of who I am.

EXERCISE 3 React to the Paragraph

Answer the following questions to show your understanding of ordering support within a paragraph.

1. What order of development does the writer use for her paragraph? __________

____

2. Could the ideas be arranged in another way? Explain. ____________________

____

3. Does the paragraph appeal to the factual reader? Imaginative reader? Explain. ______________________________

____

____

____

____

____

Work on Writing Assignment 3

EXERCISE 4 Prewrite, Plan, and Draft

Part A

Make a list of possible answers to the question "Who am I?" Jot down words that can be connected in some way next to the ones you wrote first.

____

____

____

____

____

____

____

____

Part B

In an outline plan, organize your ideas using chronological order or order of importance.

Part C

Use your outline to write a draft of your paragraph.

Building Language Skills

Vocabulary

EXERCISE 5 Use the Dictionary

Write the dictionary meanings of *close*.

____

____

____

____

____

____

____

Underline the dictionary definition of the word as it is used in the sentence.

"But as ***close*** as I was, he would never speak of the Indian blood that showed so strongly in him."

EXERCISE 6 Use the Thesaurus

Explain how the meaning of the phrase changes with the use of each synonym.

"I was a small child, often alone and often **bullied.**"

1. **. . . bullied** ____
2. **. . . persecuted** ____
3. **. . . threatened** ____
4. **. . . terrorized** ____

Precise Words

English has the largest number of synonyms of any language, yet many Americans resort to using just a few favorite expressions when they speak or write. Finding new words in a dictionary or thesaurus is an excellent way to build a vocabulary to help you write with greater flexibility, clarity, and forcefulness.

Notice how a precise word used as the subject of a sentence clarifies sentence meaning.

His **remark** surprised me.

His **report** surprised me.

His **reprimand** surprised me.

His **letter** surprised me.

One precise word can take the place of two or more words.

a **pleasant neighbor**	**unpleasant neighbor**
confidant/confidante	gossip
ally	scoundrel
advocate	freeloader
friend	nag
enthusiast	busybody

A precise verb makes the sound clear.

A fire bell **rings.** ⟶ A fire bell ***clangs.***

A sleigh bell **rings.** ⟶ A sleigh bell ***jingles.***

A church bell **rings.** ⟶ A church bell ***peals.***

A door bell **rings.** ⟶ A door bell ***chimes.***

EXERCISE 7 Identify Differences among Words

Tell how each word is different in meaning from the others in the group.

1. teenager ______________________________

   adolescent ______________________________

   juvenile ______________________________

   youth ______________________________

2. novel ______________________________

   text ______________________________

   best-seller ______________________________

   classic ______________________________

EXERCISE 8 Find Specific Words

List three synonyms for each word. Be ready to clarify the meaning of each.

1. father ______________________________
2. friend ______________________________
3. school ______________________________

Carefully chosen verbs give life and power to sentences. Precise verbs express specific actions.

ways to walk		**ways to make sound**	
sprint	strut	scream	groan
tiptoe	saunter	whisper	mutter
hop	gallop	whistle	grumble
limp	toddle	gasp	chuckle

Words provide meaning that make your thoughts clear to your reader. Make words work for you by choosing them carefully.

EXERCISE 9 Choose Precise Verbs

List two verbs that make the meaning of each given verb more specific. Be ready to give the meaning for each word.

EXAMPLE

read a book skim, study

1. **go up** a ladder ______
2. **see** the mountains ______
3. **like** telling about ______
4. **get** the meaning ______

EXERCISE 10 Write Sentences Using Precise Words

Rewrite each sentence in two different ways using precise words.

EXAMPLE

The person drove up the street in a car.

The retiree speeded up the highway in a van.

The teenager cruised around the block in a sedan.

1. The person walked into the school.

______

______

______

2. The animal ate some food.

______

______

______

3. The gift cost a lot of money.

Sentence Style

EXERCISE 11 Rearrange Sentences

Rewrite each sentence using the indicated new beginning. Be sure to keep the meaning of the original sentence. Consider the effect of rearranging the words.

1. My grandfather joked when he called me a "mongrel."

   Jokingly, ______

2. I inherited that fearlessness about high places from my grandfather.

   From my grandfather ______

3. In English, a *metis* becomes "Translator's Son."

   A metis *becomes* ______

4. The story was recited about me so often that it became inseparably associated with my thoughts of childhood.

   So often was the story ______________________________

   ____

   ____

EXERCISE 12 Combine Sentences

Combine the ideas from the sentences in each group to write one new sentence. As you write each sentence, consider the emphasis and relationships you want to achieve.

1.

I was seven.

I decided to grow up big.

I decided to grow up strong.

____

____

____

2.

My grandfather was left alone.

I was left alone.

We were left alone in the old house.

____

____

____

3.

I still love high places.

I still love cliffs and trees.

I still love resounding waterfalls.

____

____

____

4.

I was raised in the foothills of the Adirondack Mountains.

I was raised near a town.

The spring waters of the town were regarded as sacred.

____

____

____

Revising the Paragraph

EXERCISE 13 Rework for Content, Structure, and Accuracy

Part A

Revise your draft by checking to see that the support you have written follows the order of your plan. Determine if you need to rearrange the order of any of your sentences. Do you need to add sentences or omit sentences? At this point, you may need to write a second draft.

Part B

Reread your paragraph to find at least two words that can be made more precise. Circle each word. Write both the circled word and the more precise word in the left margin of your draft. When you write your final draft, choose which words to use.

Part C

Using the changes you made in your draft, write a final copy of your paragraph.

Proofread your paper to correct misspelled words, typographical errors, and missing words.

CHAPTER 4

Accomplishments

Accomplishments: Exploring the Theme

In the early twentieth century when ready-made clothing first became available in stores, many people were impressed by the new technology and yearned to buy their own outfits "off the rack." Hand-made items were often regarded as inferior to the mass-produced goods filling the marketplace. Today, although high-quality, mass-produced goods are readily available, many people take pride in their own work. The author of the selection in Chapter 4 tells about a family member who perfected a product he made by hand.

EXERCISE 1 Prepare to Read

1. What motivates a person to make something by hand? ________________

____

2. Why is a handcrafted item often more appealing than a mass-produced one?

____

____

Mount Allegro by Jerre Mangione

ABOUT THE AUTHOR

Jerre Mangione says that flunking physics is one of the best things that ever happened to him. His lack of success in science freed him to follow his aspirations as a writer. In addition to working in publishing, government, and public relations, he taught writing and wrote eleven books. In his autobiography *Mount Allegro,* Mangione tells about the Italian-American neighborhood in Rochester, New York, where he grew up during the 1920s.

---

1 Great-Uncle Minicuzzu and my Uncles Luigi and Nino were avid[1] guests at nearly every banquet my father gave. They flanked him at both sides of the table, like the disciples of Christ at the Last Supper, and they partook of his wine and cooking as though each meal were their last one.

2 There was a banquet for as many occasions as my father could imagine, and his imagination was fertile. He once gave a banquet for some relatives

[1] **avid** eager

who were moving to California and, when they were suddenly obliged to change their plans, he gave another banquet to celebrate their staying. He no sooner had finished with one banquet than he began to talk about the next one. He had the pride of an artist in his cooking, particularly his pastry making, and he never denied the story that when the Baron Michele, the richest man in the province of Girgenti, went on his honeymoon to Palermo, he took my father along to prepare his favorite desserts.

3 He was especially noted for a Sicilian delicacy[2] called *cannolo,* which was unsurpassed[3] by any of the other pastry cooks in Rochester and seldom equaled even in New York and Palermo. As a boy he had been apprenticed to a famous Sicilian pastry cook, and he learned his trade well. He might have become a celebrated pastry maker had he remained in Sicily, but here in America, the land of ice cream and pie, there was not enough of a market for his products, and he became another factory worker, expressing his real talents on holidays and other occasions when he could give banquets for his friends and relatives.

4 Although his *cannoli* were masterpieces, his recipe for making them was no secret, and he willingly itemized it for anyone who wanted to attempt it. Needless to say, no one ever approached his results, though several of his more determined imitators came to his kitchen to watch every move and measurement he made. The ingredients were simple: cottage cheese refined to a smooth paste; tiny bits of chocolate mixed into the paste; and a few drops of a magical spirit known as cannela (a liquid cinnamon), whose sharp odor recurs[4] to me with fully as many memories as a cup of tea ever gave Proust. The trick, my father claimed, was not so much in concocting the cream as in preparing the crisp, cylindrical shells that held it.

5 Like most good art, the cannoli looked simple but entailed much more work than would seem necessary to a layman. So that he would have no distractions, my father often started making his cannoli at three in the morning. Until dawn, he hovered over the shells like an anxious mother, nursing them to their proper crispness. After the shells were done, there were almonds to be roasted and crushed into golden crumbs that would be sprinkled over the ends of the cannoli once they were filled with cream. And always there had to be perfect timing. Judging from the amount of patience cannoli required and the small amount my father usually showed, he must have saved a little patience every day so that he would have enough to make his cannoli once or twice a year.

[2] **delicacy** something pleasing and appealing, especially a choice food

[3] **unsurpassed** not exceeded, unequaled

[4] **recurs** happens, comes up, or shows up again or repeatedly

6 The more enthusiasts his cannoli bred, the less inclined he was to make them. His explanation was that since he did not have time to make cannoli for all his friends and relatives, he would make them for no one but his immediate family. When occasionally he broke this rule, our house would take on the atmosphere of a secret underground society.

7 My father would solemnly[5] warn us not to tell anyone he was making cannoli. When they were finished, he would count them out carefully into empty shoeboxes he hoarded[6] for such occasions. He would then sneak them to favored relatives and friends, the right number for each family, begging them not to say a word about the gift to anyone lest someone take offense at being left out.

8 He never took money for his cannoli and would be hurt if anyone tried to pay him. Once he opened a pastry shop and featured cannoli as his specialty. For a few months business seemed good; many Sicilians bought many cannoli. Yet my father made no money. It was not until he closed the shop that he realized he had failed to charge enough to cover the cost of the ingredients.

9 In those few months he was in business, scores of new cannoli addicts were born, and ever afterward, they telephoned hopefully a week before an important holiday like Christmas or Easter to ask if Don Peppino would make a few dozen cannoli for them. He enjoyed answering the telephone at such times, even though his answer was usually no, for like any good artist it heartened him to know that his product was still appreciated and in demand.

EXERCISE 2 Reflect on What You Have Read

Finding Facts

1. What was Jerre Mangione's father's name? ______________________________

____

Making Inferences

2. Why is it that, although the father willingly shared his recipe, no other cannoli were as good as his? ______________________________

____

[5] **solemnly** seriously

[6] **hoarded** stored for future use; stashed, accumulated, or stockpiled

Sharing Reactions

3. Should the father have accepted money for his cannoli? Explain.

FOCUSING ON Transitions

Just as a motorist has a difficult time getting from place to place without appropriate traffic signals and road signs, a reader has a difficult time getting from idea to idea without directions. Directions in writing are provided with transitions, signals that link one idea to another.

Transition words, pronouns, repetition of words, and synonyms are used for transition.

Transition Words

Transition words are words showing connections between parts of sentences, sentences, or paragraphs.

To show addition

My father warned us not tell anyone he was cooking. **Furthermore,** when he was finished, he sneaked them to favored relatives and friends.

To show contrast

For a few months business seemed good, **yet** my father made no money.

To show similarity

Like most good art, the cannoli looked simple but entailed much more work.

To show time order

Subsequently, he opened a pastry shop and featured his specialty.

To show space order

At almost every banquet, my great uncles sat **next** to my father.

To show a change in direction

Although he was a master pastry cook, here in America, there was not enough of a market for his products.

To show cause and effect

He failed to charge enough money to cover the cost of ingredients. **Consequently,** he had to close the shop.

To show emphasis

Indeed, no one ever approached his results.

To show illustration

The ingredients were simple. **For example,** he used cottage cheese, tiny bits of chocolate, and cannela.

To show summary or clarification

After all, it heartened him to know that his product was appreciated and in demand.

Pronouns

Pronouns, words that take the place of nouns, are useful in linking ideas. Notice how the pronouns provide effective transition in the following sentences:

Great-Uncle Minicuzzu and my Uncles Luigi and Nino were avid guests at nearly every banquet my **father** gave. ***They*** flanked ***him*** at both sides of the table.

TRANSITION WORD CHART

To show addition	also, next, another, and, in addition, moreover, further, furthermore, finally, besides, and then, likewise, nor, too, again, equally important, last, incidentally
To show contrast	but, yet, however, still, nevertheless, on the other hand, on the contrary, even so, in contrast to, at the same time, although this may be true, otherwise, nonetheless, instead
To show similarity	like, likewise, similarly
To show time order	first, then, next, after, as, before, while, meanwhile, soon, now, during, finally, subsequently, at the same time
To show space order	here, beyond, nearby, below, opposite to, adjacent to, on the opposite side of, nearby, across, to the left, to the right, next to
To show a change in direction	but, however, yet, in contrast, although, otherwise, still, on the contrary, on the other hand
To show a relationship of cause and effect	therefore, consequently, as a result
To show emphasis	indeed, in fact, without a doubt
To show illustration	for example, for instance, that is, in other words, specifically, such as
To show summary or clarification	in summary, in conclusion, in brief, after all

Repetition of Key Words

The repetition of a key word can connect sentences.

> There was a **banquet** for as many occasions as my father could imagine, and his imagination was fertile. He once gave a **banquet** for some relatives who were moving to California, and when they were suddenly obliged to change their plans, he gave another **banquet** to celebrate their staying. He no sooner had finished with one **banquet** than he began to talk about the next one.

Synonyms

Rather than repeat a key word over and over, it is often more effective to use a synonym, a word that means nearly the same as the key word, to show a connection between one idea and another.

> Apprenticed to **a famous pastry cook,** my father learned many secrets. The ***baker*** taught my father how to make a paper-thin cannoli shell.

Use a variety of transitions

Using a variety of transitions makes the relationship among ideas clear and thoughts flow smoothly from one point to the next.

Developing a Paragraph

Assignment 4: Writing about Accomplishments

Jerre Mangione writes about his father's skill as a pastry maker. Don Peppino's accomplishment brought him personal pride and gave pleasure to the many people who enjoyed eating his cannoli. Jerre Mangione himself demonstrates an accomplishment as an author. He is able to use words to bring his father to life. Most people have reason to be proud of something they have accomplished. The achievement could be creating a project or meeting a goal individually or as part of a group. Often accomplishments are made in the area of the arts, such as making a wonderful dessert or writing a book, or in athletics, such as making the winning goal or staying with an exercise program. They may be achieved on the job, such as mastering a skill or surviving a busy season, or in the area of life skills, such as giving up a bad habit or handling a difficult situation well.

Think about what you or someone you know has accomplished. What is the accomplishment? Did this accomplishment take place at home? At work? In the neighborhood? At school? As part of an organization? How much time, effort, or patience was involved? Did this accomplishment result in a sense of pride? Pleasure? Relief? Or did it have some other results?

For Writing Assignment 4, write a paragraph telling about an accomplishment that you or someone you know has experienced.

The Writing Process

Questioning

Prewriting Techniques

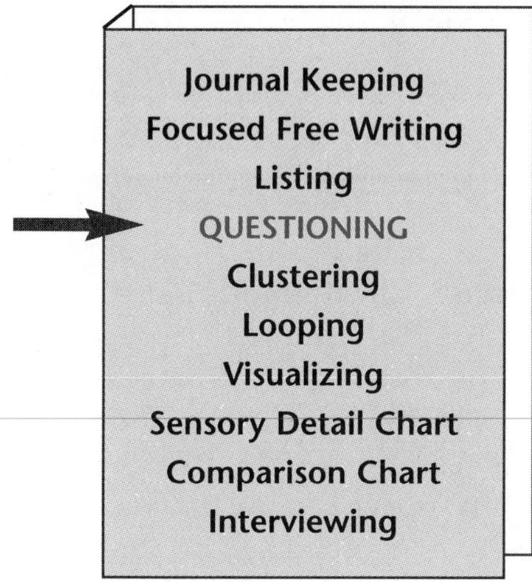

You can gather ideas by asking the same questions that reporters often use when they are getting facts for a story: ***Who? What? Where? When? Why?*** Look at an example using the **five W questions:**

Who is the person who accomplished something?

My friend's father, Joe

What did the person accomplish?

He caught an eight-pound large-mouth bass.

Where did the person accomplish this?

He caught the fish on Seneca Lake.

When did the person accomplish this?

He caught the fish last summer.

Why/How did the person accomplish this?

He has the equipment and know-how.

A Paragraph Plan

Following is an outline of a paragraph based on the answers to the W questions given earlier.

Topic Sentence My friend's father, Joe caught an eight-pound large-mouth bass last summer on Seneca Lake.

1. Major point	1. persistent fisherman
a. Supporting detail	a. fishes every weekend
b. Supporting detail	b. usually catches little fish
c. Supporting detail	c. fishes in all kinds of weather
2. Major point	2. favorite location
Supporting detail	shallow end
3. Major point	3. big fish
a. Supporting detail	a. hard struggle
b. Supporting detail	b. reeled in the large-mouth bass

A Model Paragraph

Read the following paragraph written from the outline.

THE BIG CATCH

My friend's father, Joe, caught an eight-pound large-mouth bass last summer on Seneca Lake. Beer-bellied and middle-aged, Joe is one of the most enthusiastic fishermen I've met. Every weekend during the fishing season, he's out on his boat hoping for the big catch. Usually he lands a few perch, small-mouth bass, or a trout, but never the big catch. One hot, hazy day last August, not really a good day for fishing, Joe, ever optimistic, went fishing. He headed his boat to the shallow end of the lake where there were many trees and water lilies near the shore. Placing his favorite bass lure on his line, he cast into those places the fish like to hide. After just a few casts, the big fish hit his lure really hard, almost jerking the rod out of his hand. Quickly, he recovered and began the difficult task of reeling this monstrous fish into his boat. The bass alternately dived and leaped, desperately trying to lose the hook, but the lure was firmly lodged in the huge mouth. After about five minutes of fighting, Joe was able to reel in the tiring fish. At last, the exhausted fish was next to the boat. Triumphantly using his net, Joe landed his large-mouth bass.

EXERCISE 3 React to the Paragraph

Answer the following questions to show your understanding of paragraph support and the use of transitions.

1. What details does the writer provide for factual, imaginative, and curious readers? ______

2. What word is effectively repeated in the paragraph? ______

3. What synonyms are used for "fish"? ______________________________

____

4. What transition words are used to show time order? ______________

____

____

Work on Writing Assignment 4

EXERCISE 4 Prewrite, Plan, and Draft

Part A

Answer the five W questions about your topic.

Who is the person who has accomplished something?______________

What has the person accomplished?______________________________

Where did/does the person accomplish this? ______________________

When did/does the person accomplish this?_______________________

Why/How has the person been able to accomplish this? ____________

____

____

____

____

Part B

Write a topic sentence and outline plan for your paragraph.

Part C

Use your outline plan to write a draft of your paragraph. Give your paragraph a title.

Building Language Skills

Vocabulary

EXERCISE 5 Use the Dictionary

Write dictionary definitions for the word *score.*

____

____

____

____

____

____

____

____

Underline the definition of the word as it is used in the sentence.

"In those few months he was in business, ***scores*** of new cannoli addicts were born. . . ."

EXERCISE 6 Use the Thesaurus

Explain how the meaning of the phrase changes with the use of each synonym.

"Great-Uncle Minicuzzu and my Uncles Luigi and Nino were ***avid*** guests at nearly every banquet my father gave."

1. *avid* guests ____
2. *voracious* guests ____
3. *greedy* guests ____

4. *anxious* guests ______________________________

5. *enthusiastic* guests ______________________________

Simple Sentences

What is a simple sentence?

A **simple sentence** is a group of words containing a subject-verb combination that makes sense when written alone. Another name for a simple sentence is **independent clause.**

A simple sentence can be any length.

My **father** made no money.

My Italian-born, fifty-year old **father** made no money from all his hours baking in the pastry shop.

A sentence can include one subject with *two verbs* related to that subject.

Once **he** opened a pastry shop and featured cannoli as his specialty.

A sentence can also contain *two subjects* and one verb.

Great-Uncle Minicuzzu and **Uncle Luigi** sat next to my father.

Or, a simple sentence may have *two or more subjects* and *two or more verbs.*

Great-Uncle Minicuzzu and **Uncle Luigi** sat and ate with my father.

Note: When a sentence has a subject + verb combination followed by another subject + verb combination, the sentence is no longer called a simple sentence. It is a **compound** or a **complex** or a **compound-complex sentence.** You learn more about these sentences in later chapters.

S V + S V

He would be hurt if **anyone** tried to pay him.

Sentence Fragments

What is a sentence fragment?

A **sentence fragment** is a group of words that is incorrectly punctuated as a complete sentence.

As you know, a sentence must have a subject-verb combination. A sentence must also stand alone; that is, it must be independent or make sense by itself.

One kind of sentence fragment is a phrase or a group of words that does not contain a subject-verb combination.

made no money

fifty-year-old father

from all his hours

A second kind of sentence fragment is a dependent clause, a group of words with a subject-verb combination that does not make sense by itself.

as though each meal were their last one

although several of his more determined imitators came to his kitchen

because his *cannoli* were masterpieces

when they were suddenly obliged to change their plans

Some of the common words that begin dependent clauses are

after	because	provided that	until
although	before	since	when
as	even though	so that	where
as if	if		than
as long as	once	though	whether
as though			wherever

How can sentence fragments be corrected?

Written alone, a phrase or dependent clause is called a **sentence fragment.** You can correct a sentence fragment either by rewriting it to create a sentence or by joining it with a sentence that comes before or after it. To be used appropriately, a phrase or dependent clause needs to be part of a complete sentence. Note the italicized fragments in the following writing:

Incorrect

He enjoyed answering the telephone at such times. *Even though his answer was usually, "No."*

For like any good artist. It heartened him to know. *That his product was still appreciated and in demand.*

Often, you can correct a fragment by attaching it to a sentence that comes before or after it.

Correct

He enjoyed answering the telephone at such times *even though his answer was usually, "No."*

For like any good artist, it heartened him to know *that his product was still appreciated and in demand.*

Another type of fragment occurs when either the subject or verb is missing from a sentence. In this case, add a subject or verb to the fragment to create a complete sentence.

Incorrect

My father hovering over the shells.

or

Couldn't keep his business going.

To correct these fragments add a subject or verb.

Correct

v

My father **was** hovering over the shells.

s
↓

He couldn't keep his business going.

EXERCISE 7 Write Complete Sentences

Add a subject, verb, or both to make a complete sentence. Write the sentence on the line provided.

EXAMPLE

to learn the secret ingredients.

His neighbors wanted to learn the secret ingredients.

1. to watch his every move and measurement

____

2. solemnly warn us

____

3. after the banquet

____

4. answering the telephone at such times

____

5. my father making his cannoli at three in the morning

____

6. cannoli for all his friends and relatives

____

7. to beg them not to say a word about the gift to anyone

____

8. was still appreciated and in demand

____

9. for many years after

____

10. the richest man on his honeymoon to Palermo

____

Run-on Sentences

What are run-on sentences?

Independent clauses or sentences written one after another and not properly punctuated are called **run-on sentences** or **fused sentences.** For accuracy and ease of communication, individual sentences must be punctuated properly.

You will probably have difficulty reading the following words with no sentence divisions.

He never took money for his cannoli and would be hurt if anyone tried to pay him once he opened a pastry shop and featured cannoli as his specialty for a few months business seemed good many Sicilians bought many cannoli yet my father made no money it was not until he closed the shop that he realized he had failed to charge enough to cover the cost of the ingredients.

Here are the words rewritten as sentences, making the sentences easier to read.

He never took money for his cannoli and would be hurt if anyone tried to pay him. Once he opened a pastry shop and featured cannoli as his specialty. For a few months business seemed good; many Sicilians bought many cannoli. Yet my father made no money. It was not until he closed the shop that he realized he had failed to charge enough to cover the cost of the ingredients.

EXERCISE 8 Edit for Sentences

Label each of the following: F for fragment, R for run-on sentence, or S for correct sentence. Correct the sentence fragments and run-on sentences on the lines provided.

_______ 1. Like most good art, making the cannoli looked simple.

____

____

_______ 2. That he would have no distractions.

_______ 3. My father often started baking at three in the morning until dawn he hovered over the shells like an anxious mother, nursing them to their proper crispness.

_______ 4. After the shells were done, there were almonds to be roasted and crushed into golden crumbs.

_______ 5. The golden crumbs were sprinkled over the ends of the cannoli they were filled with cream.

_______ 6. Judging from the amount of patience cannoli required and the small amount my father usually showed.

_______ 7. Entailed much more work than would seem necessary to a layman.

_______ 8. He must have saved a little patience every day.

Sentence Style

EXERCISE 9 Rearrange Sentences

Rewrite each sentence using the indicated new beginning. Keep the meaning of the original sentence. Be able to explain the effect of rearranging the words.

1. Great-Uncle Minicuzzu and my Uncles Luigi and Nino were avid guests at nearly every banquet my father gave.

   At nearly every banquet ______________________________

   ____

   ____

2. There was a banquet for as many occasions as my father could imagine.

   A banquet ______________________________

   ____

   ____

3. He expressed his real talents on holidays and other occasions when we gave banquets for friends and relatives.

   One way he expressed his real talents ______________________________

   ____

   ____

4. My father would solemnly warn us not to tell anyone.

   We ______________________________

   ____

   ____

EXERCISE 10 Combine Sentences

Combine the ideas from the sentences in each group to write one new sentence. As you write each sentence, consider the emphasis and relationships you want to achieve.

1\.

He gave a banquet for relatives.

The relatives were moving to California.

______

______

______

2\.

My father was young.

My father was apprenticed to a pastry cook.

______

______

______

3\.

The pastry cook was famous.

The pastry cook was Sicilian.

______

______

______

4.

Baron Michele was the richest man in the province of Girgenti.

The Baron went on his honeymoon.

The Baron took my father along.

5.

One ingredient is cannela.

Cannela is a liquid cinnamon.

Revising the Paragraph

EXERCISE 11 Rework for Content, Structure, and Accuracy

Part A

Reread your draft to find where you have used transitions to help your reader follow your ideas. If needed, add transitions. Use a different color pen or font to indicate the transitions you used.

Part B

Reread your draft to make sure you have a subject-verb combination in every sentence and that sentences are punctuated appropriately. Correct any errors you find.

Part C

Using the revisions you made on your draft, write a final copy of your paragraph. Proofread your paper to correct misspelled words, typographical errors, and missing words.

PART TWO

Essay Writing

CHAPTER 5

Priorities

Priorities: Exploring the Theme

What things do you treasure? Are they things that have material value? Or, are they things that have no monetary price? A thoughtful consideration of your possessions will show something about your priorities or what is important to you. These priorities help define who you are. The author of the reading selection in Chapter 5 shows not only what is important to her but also what is *most* important to her.

EXERCISE 1 Prepare to Read

1. What things are often important to people?

____

____

2. Tell about a time when something important to you was lost or broken.

____

____

And the Bridge Is Love by Faye Moskowitz

ABOUT THE AUTHOR

Faye Moskowitz was raised as part of a large, close Jewish family living in Depression-era Michigan. As an adult, she interweaves stories of her childhood with those of her adult life as teacher, activist, parent, and writer. An important theme for her is that adults must pay attention to children and talk to them. In addition to *And the Bridge is Love,* Moskowitz has written *Whoever Finds This: I Love You* and *A Leak in the Heart: Personal Essays and Life Stories.*

---

1 For years after the Depression, my immigrant parents paid off debts, rebuilding financial security dollar by dollar. One happy day, a delivery van replaced our old lumpy davenport[1] and sagging easy chair with spindly-legged burled maple and fruitwood furniture. One piece especially captured my imagination, a glass-shelved and velvet-lined curio[2] cabinet that stood on curved legs as delicate as a thoroughbred's.

[1] **davenport** a long couch with a back and ends

[2] **curio** antique, relic, heirloom

2 Inside the cabinet, my mother kept a collection of small English bone china cups, each gold-rimmed and banded in a different jewel-like color. Perhaps to her the tiny cups symbolized an end to want and economic insecurity. I know she loved them. She made a ceremony of washing them each week, using a heavy Turkish towel to cushion the translucent[3] china in the porcelain sink.

3 Clara, who helped my mother, was gingerly[4] dusting the curio cabinet with a feather duster one afternoon when she knocked over a cup and broke off its handle. I had been reading nearby and saw her crying as she carried the two fragments of china to my mother. I thought Clara wept for the pretty cup. I didn't know then that she feared she might be fired. Hard times were still more than a memory for many in those days.

4 My mother blanched[5] when she realized what lay in Clara's hands. But after a few moments she said, "In our family we call this kind of accident a *kapore.*" She reached out and took the pieces, cradling them in her palm. "You see, the broken cup takes the place of harm that might have come to one of us. Don't cry, Clara," she said, "everything can be replaced except a human life."

5 My mother died not many years after that. The collection of dainty cups came to me, and I gave them a place of honor in my first home. I think I loved them even more than my mother had; their beauty was bound up with her memory. They sat on a small wooden shelf in my bedroom—eleven perfect cups and one with a mended handle. I, too, washed them as my mother had, cushioning the kitchen sink with a folded bath towel. I allowed no one to touch the cups but me. Sometimes I would take them down, one by one, to show to my little daughter. I told her that the tiny cups with their brilliant bands of color would someday belong to her.

6 One winter morning while I worked in another part of the house, my daughter climbed on a chair to reach the cups. She must have lost her balance. By the time I heard the crash, she lay on the floor, the shelf on top of her. Of the cups, only a profusion of bright colored shards[6] remained.

7 Heart pounding, I snatched up my howling child and frantically felt her head for bumps. I peered into her streaming eyes. Had she been cut or even blinded by flying glass? When I determined that she wasn't really hurt, I took her on my lap. As in a dream, my mother's words came back to me.

[3] **translucent** transparent, clear, glassy

[4] **gingerly** carefully, cautiously

[5] **blanched** paled, turned white

[6] **shards** pieces, chips

"Those were only china cups," I crooned[7], rocking my daughter back and forth. "They can be replaced. Only you, my precious, cannot be replaced."

• • •

Some time after the cups are broken, the author experienced another loss.

• • •

8 Many years later, my husband and I drove to our house the day after the fire, grateful to find much of it still standing. In the dimly lit shambles of that once-perfect bedroom, I felt my way through splintered wood and broken glass until my fingers touched a sodden bundle of cloth. Hugging the quilt to my breast, I carried it into the sunshine and spread it on the grass. Half-covered in soot and reeking of the fire that had almost consumed it, a corner of the quilt survived, its luminous triangles still triumphantly marching.

9 As we go about the tedious task of rebuilding, I think often of the nameless woman patiently piecing scraps of pink and blue and green, a vision of perfection spurring her needle. Her lesson is that beauty and wholeness can be created from broken pieces. But broken pieces—scraps of fabric, shards of china, the ruins of a farmhouse—remind me of an even more important lesson.

10 I tell myself the quilt I cherished so is the *kapore,* the object that took the place of harm that might otherwise have come to one of us. My mother's lesson is the most significant of all, for no material thing, no matter how beloved, can ever have the value of a human life.

EXERCISE 2 Reflect on What You Have Read

Finding Facts

1. How many china cups were in the original set? ______________________

____

Making Inferences

2. Why does the author believe in a *kapore?* ______________________

____

____

____

[7] **crooned** murmured in a low voice

Sharing Reactions

3. Did the author appropriately handle her daughter's breaking the cups? ______

____

____

____

FOCUSING ON Essay Structure

Overview of the Essay

If you were to collect some paragraphs and put them together, what you would have is a collection of paragraphs. If, on the other hand, you put together a series of paragraphs that expressed a point of view on a topic and provided an introduction for the paragraphs and a conclusion that tied the paragraphs together, then you would have an essay. The essay, composed of multiple paragraphs, can develop a topic in greater depth than a single paragraph.

In academic writing, you are asked to write essays, also called **themes** or **papers,** to share opinions and information for assignments and on exams. When an essay includes information from the library or other sources, it is called a **research paper**.

Depending on your topic, your audience, and the purpose for your writing, you can choose from a variety of methods to develop an essay. These methods include illustration, narration, description, comparison, illustration, and persuasion. The following chapters provide opportunities for you to write using each of these methods of development.

How long is an essay?

The length of an essay is determined by the assignment, the scope of the topic, and the amount of support provided. An essay in introductory writing classes typically contains about 500 words and is composed of five paragraphs—an introductory paragraph, three body paragraphs, and a concluding paragraph.

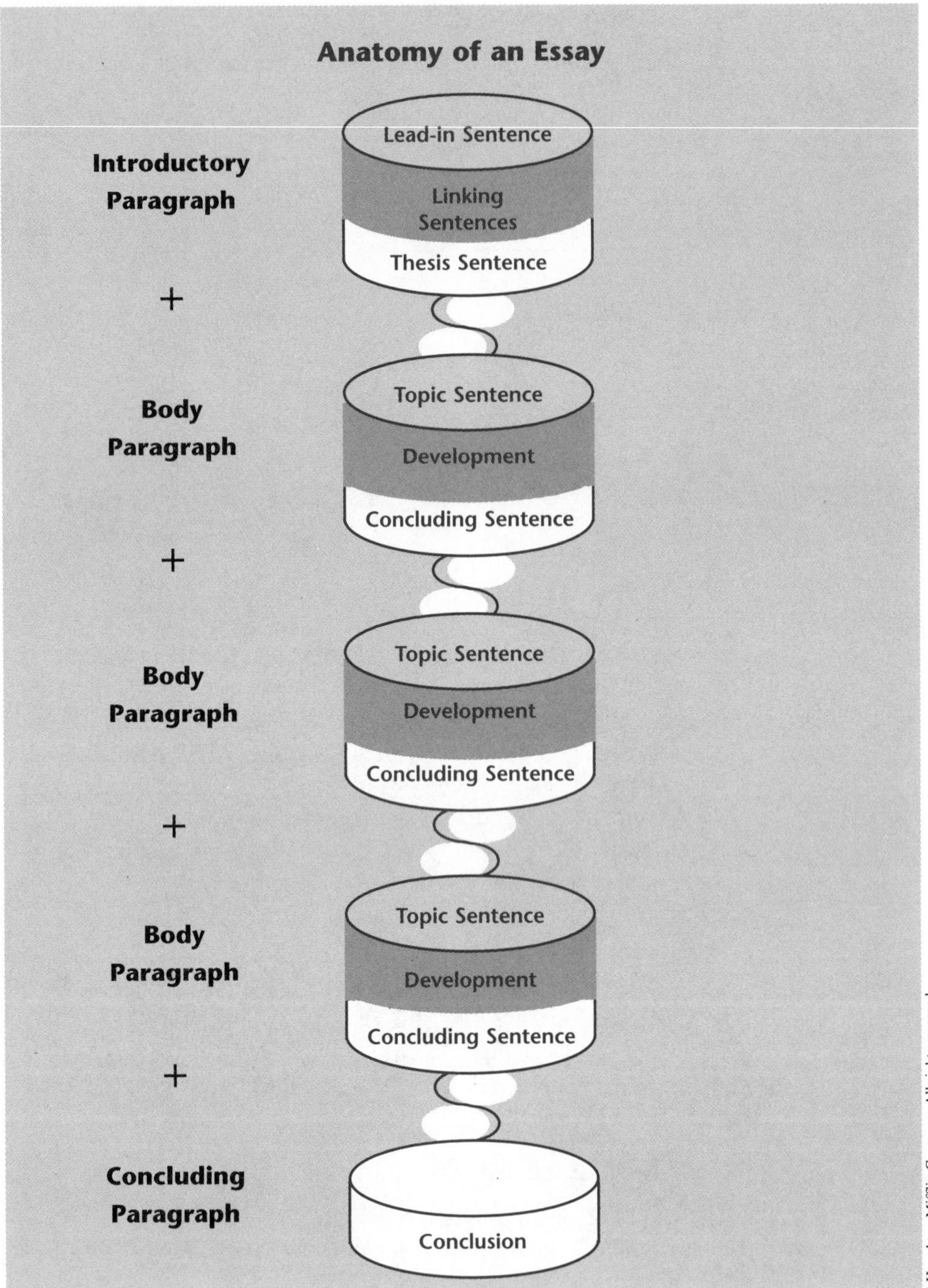
Anatomy of an Essay
Introductory Paragraph
Lead-in Sentence
Linking Sentences
Thesis Sentence
+
Body Paragraph
Topic Sentence
Development
Concluding Sentence
+
Body Paragraph
Topic Sentence
Development
Concluding Sentence
+
Body Paragraph
Topic Sentence
Development
Concluding Sentence
+
Concluding Paragraph
Conclusion

You may find, however, that some essays are effectively developed with three, four, six, or even more paragraphs.

What are the parts of an essay?

An essay, like a paragraph, has a beginning, a middle, and an end.

PARAGRAPH AND ESSAY COMPARED

	Paragraph	**Essay**
What is the structure?	introductory **sentence** body **sentences** concluding **sentence**	introductory **paragraph** body **paragraphs** concluding **paragraph**
What is the main idea sentence called?	**topic sentence**	**thesis sentence**
What is the length?	average 8–12 **sentences**	average 3–10 **paragraphs**
What prewriting techniques are used?	journal keeping, focused free writing, listing, questioning; clustering, looping, visualizing sensory details, comparison charting, interviewing	
How are ideas ordered?	order of importance chronological order spatial order	

Like a paragraph, an essay is based on a topic. Sometimes this topic is assigned or is a test question. Other times you select a topic that you know about or are interested in. After you determine the topic for your essay, you want to decide your opinion about the topic. This statement of your opinion is called a **thesis**.

Thesis

Just as a topic sentence states the main idea developed in a paragraph, a **thesis sentence** states the main idea developed in an essay. A thesis includes a topic and a reaction, which may be an opinion, an attitude, a belief, or a point of view.

Example

thesis = topic + opinion

↓ ↓

Several of my **possessions** provide me with **independence.**

To be sure you have stated an opinion, a helpful technique is to write in parenthesis the words **I believe** or **I feel** in front of the sentence. (These words do not appear in the final copy of your essay.) Check to see that the statement makes sense.

(I believe) Several of my possessions provide me with independence.

What is the controlling question?

Turn your thesis sentence into a question. This is the **controlling question** for your essay. Can you answer the question? If you can, you know that you have support for the development of the body of the essay.

Example

Thesis: Several possessions provide me with independence.

The **controlling question** can be stated in a number of ways.

How do my most important possessions provide me with independence?

Why do my most important possessions provide me with independence?

My cellular telephone helps me to be in contact with others wherever I am.

My motorbike enables me to go places on my own.

My computer allows me to work on my own.

These answers to the question are the support for the essay. Each of the answers can be written as a topic sentence for a body paragraph.

If you restate your thesis sentence as a question but you cannot answer the question, you will have difficulty writing an essay based on that thesis. Try rewriting your thesis sentence and controlling question.

How is a thesis focused?

Similar to a topic sentence, a thesis sentence must be appropriately focused. Consider this potential thesis: *I value the possessions in my house.* The sentence has a topic, *the possessions in my house,* and a focus, *I value.* Developing this thesis, however, is a project far too large for a single essay. It could take pages to tell about the many things in your house and why you consider them *of value.* The sentence is too broad to be an effective thesis for an essay.

A narrower focus, *I value the possessions in my room,* is probably still too broad to be a thesis for an essay, even one with five paragraphs.

An effective thesis is *I value my guitar.* This thesis expresses a clear, focused belief about the topic, *possessions.*

BROAD: I value the possessions in my house.

NARROWED: **I value the possessions in my room.**

THESIS: I value my guitar.

A **controlling question** for this thesis is

How is my guitar of value to me?

or

Why do I value my guitar?

Thesis Sentence with Essay Map

I value my guitar because I use it for composing songs, entertaining friends, and simply relaxing.

EXERCISE 3 Analyze Effective Thesis Statements

Write T next to those sentences that would make an effective thesis. Be ready to explain your answer.

_______ 1. There are many things in my house that are important to me.
_______ 2. My journal reveals parts of my personality.
_______ 3. I am going to write about things I value.
_______ 4. I don't really have a favorite possession.
_______ 5. Three of my favorite possessions remind me of people I love.
_______ 6. People have many different types of possessions.
_______ 7. I like to wear my special bracelet on my left arm.
_______ 8. My computer is essential to my education.
_______ 9. The keys to my car represent my busy life.
_______ 10. My grandfather's dog tags from the Vietnam War have meaning for him.
_______ 11. The kitchen table at our house brings back memories of growing up.
_______ 12. A cell phone helps me make it through the day.
_______ 13. My neighbor has a variety of gardening tools.
_______ 14. What possessions do I need?
_______ 15. The ticket stubs in my wallet remind me of good times.
_______ 16. The belongings I keep in my book bag have special importance.
_______ 17. I treasure my high school year book.

What is an essay map?

Sometimes, you may want to add an "essay map" to your thesis sentence. Much as a road map gives an overview of geographical places, an essay map gives an overview of the major points in an essay.

Thesis: My favorite possessions reflect my passion for technology.

Essay map written as a sentence following a thesis:

My favorite possessions reflect my passion for technology. I cannot imagine my life without my answering machine, my pager, and my remote control.

Thesis including essay map:

My favorite possessions, including my answering machine, pager, and remote control, reflect my passion for technology.

or

Favorite possessions of mine that reflect my passion for technology are my answering machine, pager, and remote control.

EXERCISE 4 Write a Thesis, Controlling Question, and Essay Map

Select five topics. For each, prewrite to gather some ideas, and then write a working thesis and controlling question. For two of the topics, include an essay map.

teenage curfew

dress code

TV talk shows

leisure time

commuting

living in dormitory/apartment

day care

peer pressure

computer literacy

military

Topic #1 ____

Thesis ____

____

Controlling Question ____

Topic #2 ____________________

Thesis ____________________

____

Controlling Question ____________________

Topic #3 ____________________

Thesis ____________________

____

Controlling Question ____________________

Topic #4 ____________________

Thesis ____________________

____

Controlling Question ____________________

Essay Map ____________________

Topic #5 ____________________

Thesis ____________________

____

Controlling Question ____________________

Essay Map ____________________

Developing an Essay

Assignment 5: Writing About Priorities

Faye Moskowitz writes about a favorite possession, her china cups with their gold rims and beautifully colored bands. These cups are especially important to her because they were her mother's.

Possessions, like the china cups, can be reminders of people, places, or occasions. Things may have value because they are important for work or play. Rings or bracelets, for example, may have special significance. A camera or a math book may show what is important. A baseball mitt may represent many seasons of work and fun.

Think about some of your possessions. For each, consider: What are its physical characteristics? Is it one of a kind? Di you purchase the object? Was it given to you? Where do you keep it? How long have you had it? How is it important to you? Is the possession useful? What is its sentimental, historical, or monetary value? Which of your priorities does it represent?

For Writing Assignment 5, write an essay explaining the significance of one or more possessions.

The Writing Process

Clustering

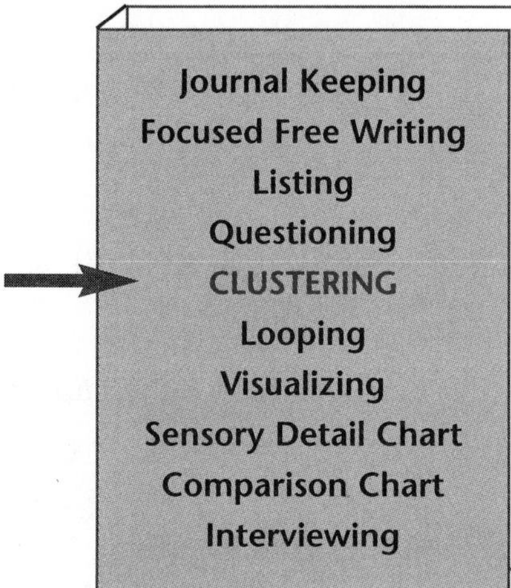

Clustering provides a visual representation of your ideas about a topic. To cluster, write the topic in the center of your paper and draw a circle around it. Then extend lines from the topic and write words that relate to it. Circle these words. Around each of these circled words, extend lines and once again, write words that relate in some way to these words. Repeat the process over and over. When you have made your diagram as full as you can, look it over to see where the most clusters and words are. These are areas on which to focus as you develop a thesis and plan an essay.

Study an example of clustering that generates ideas about possessions.

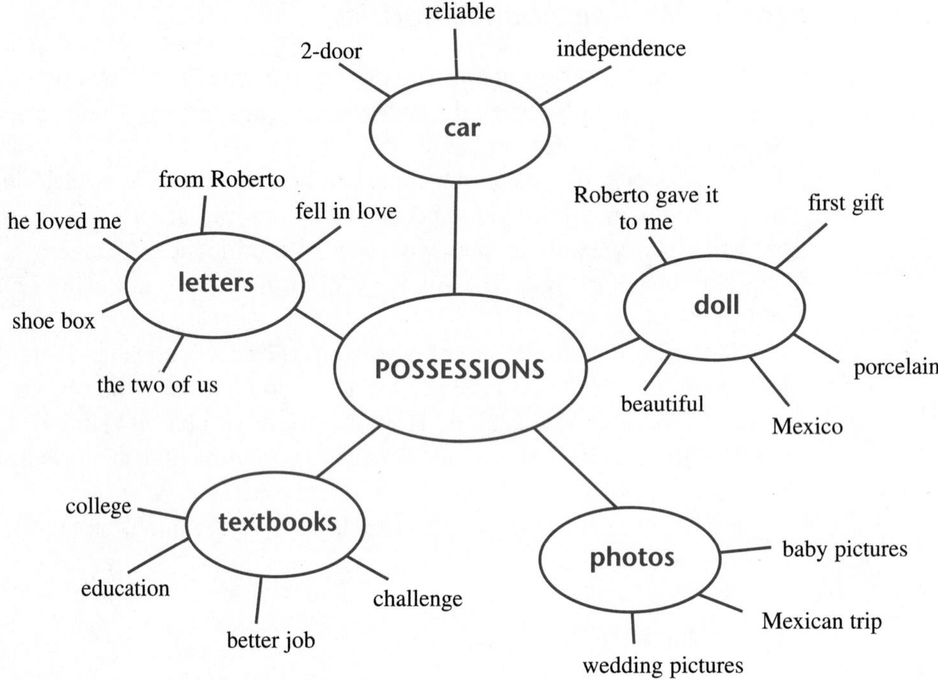

An Essay Plan

Planning an essay is similar to outlining a paragraph. You may use words, phrases, or sentences in your plan. Notice in this plan how each topic sentence supports the thesis sentence.

Thesis Sentence: Certain objects, ones that remind me of the wonderful times my husband and I once had, are dear to me.

I. Topic sentence for first body paragraph	I. I cherish the doll my husband gave me when we first met.
A. Major point	A. from Mexico
B. Major point	B. Roberto's gift
C. Major point	C. porcelain doll
D. Major point	D. beginning of our relationship

II. Topic sentence for second body paragraph
   A. Major point
   B. Major point
   C. Major point
   D. Major point

III. Topic sentence for third body paragraph
   A. Major point
   B. Major point
   C. Major point

II. I value the box of love letters my husband wrote when we were apart.
   A. couldn't call
   B. letters in a box
   C. one special letter
   D. memories of our love

III. I have precious photographs of our two babies.
   A. baby picture of my son
   B. baby picture of my daughter
   C. memory of what used to be

A Model Essay

Read an essay that illustrates what possessions are important to the writer.

A DOLL, A LETTER, AND TWO PICTURES

Introductory paragraph

1 When I was twenty years old, I fell in love with the man I was to marry. During our fifteen years together, we had two children and bought a house. Like most couples, we had good and bad times together. Recently, though, my husband and I separated. Our house, filled with decorations and furnishings, feels nearly empty. Certain objects, ones that remind me of the wonderful times my husband and I once had, are dear to me.

First body paragraph developing example #1

2 One thing that I cherish is a doll given to me after I met my husband. It was my first time away from home when my friend Lucy and I took a week's vacation in Guadalajara, Mexico. After checking into the hotel, we walked over to the taxis lined up on the street outside the hotel entrance. A tall, good-looking guy stepped out of a taxi and asked us if we needed a ride. As Roberto and I continued talking

with one another during the taxi ride, we felt an instant attraction, and we arranged to meet later that night. All during the week, Roberto was our personal tour guide. One day the three of us went to the mall, and I was captivated by the dolls in a window display of a quaint little shop. Without saying anything, Roberto went into the store and bought a beautiful porcelain doll dressed in festive Mexican attire. He gave me the doll and said, "Whenever you look at it, I hope you will think of me." From that day on, I have kept the doll in my bedroom at all times. This doll represents the beginning of a relationship with my husband and the love we felt for each other.

Second body paragraph developing example #2

3 The second thing I value is a stack of love letters that my husband wrote when we were apart. Neither of us had extra money to call, so we used to write to each other all the time. I lined a shoebox with tissue paper, and after I read Roberto's words, I would slip the letter back into its envelope and place it in the box that I kept under my bed. As months went by, it became clear that we missed each other. Each day I would go to work thinking about nothing else but whether there would be mail from Mexico. My mother would shake her head and say, "Maria, you hardly know this person. He writes only what he wants you to know." But I knew better. One day Roberto wrote me a long letter expressing what he felt for me and how much he wanted to be near me. Then I knew he wrote from his heart, and we were meant for each other. Today, when I reread his letters, I can remember the days when we first fell in love.

Third body paragraph developing example #3

4 Even more important than the doll and the letter are the precious photographs of our two babies on my dresser. The photo on the right shows our son at his first birthday party. What a wonderful time we had that day. Our dining room was filled with family and friends talking, eating, and singing. The photo on the left shows our daughter when she was a newborn. I can still remember the excitement of giving birth to a beautiful, healthy girl. In the picture, I see her

with just the hint of the sparkling dark eyes and mischievous smile that marks the energetic eight-year-old she is today. Now I have the joy of being with our two children but also the responsibility of raising them alone without a father. The photos are a memory of what used to be.

Concluding paragraph

5 When Roberto and I exchanged our marriage vows fifteen years ago, I thought our love would last forever. I thought we were a happy family. I do not understand why he cheated on me—and our children. Now my growing children are my life. A doll, a letter, and some photos are all that remain of my first love.

EXERCISE 5 React to the Essay

Answer each of the following questions to show your understanding of thesis, support, and effectiveness.

1. What is the ***controlling question*** that this essay answers? ________________

____

____

____

2. What is the ***order of development*** used in this essay? What transitions show this order of development? ________________

____

____

____

3. What details does the writer provide for factual, imaginative, and curious readers? ________________

____

____

Essay Coherence

Just as transitions make a paragraph coherent by showing how one sentence is related to the next, transitions in an essay show the interrelationship of ideas and the movement of ideas through an essay. Including transition words, repetition of words, and pronoun substitutes helps an essay flow smoothly from word to word, sentence to sentence, and paragraph to paragraph.

One way to connect body paragraphs with the thesis is to identify in the thesis sentence the **key words** that express attitude. Then find **synonyms** for this key word to use in your topic sentences.

Example

Thesis sentence:

Certain objects, ones that remind me of the wonderful times my husband and I once had, are **dear** to me.

Topic sentence # 1:

One thing that I **cherish** is a doll given to me after I first met my husband.

Topic sentence # 2:

The second thing I **value** is the stack of love letters that my husband wrote when we were apart from each other.

Topic sentence # 3:

Even more important than the doll and the letter are the **precious** photographs of our two babies I have on my dresser.

Work on Writing Assignment 5

EXERCISE 6 Prewrite, Plan, and Draft

Part A

Create a cluster about possessions that are important to you.

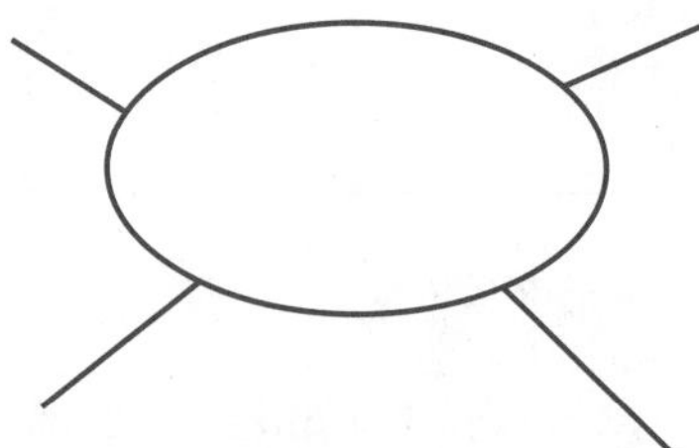

Part B

1. Use the format below to complete a plan for your essay.

Title ______________________________

Thesis sentence (essay map) ______________________________

____

____

What are the **key words** in your thesis? ______________________________

Write at least three synonyms for the key words. ______________________________

Controlling question ______________________________

Topic Sentence # 1 ______________________________

(Circle the synonym that links the topic sentence to your thesis sentence.)

a. ______________________________

b. ______________________________

c. ______________________________

Topic Sentence # 2 ______________________________

(Circle the synonym that links the topic sentence to your thesis sentence.)

a. ______________________________

b. ____________________

c. ____________________

Topic Sentence # 3 ____________________

(Circle the synonym that links the topic sentence to your thesis sentence.)

a. ____________________

b. ____________________

c. ____________________

Part C

Use your essay plan to write a draft of your essay. Since you learn more about writing the introductory and concluding paragraphs in the next chapter, you may want to write only your thesis statement and body paragraphs.

Building Language Skills

Vocabulary

Word Meanings

EXERCISE 7 Use the Dictionary

Write the definitions of the word *luminous*.

____

____

____

____

____

____

Underline the definition of the word as it is used in the reading selection.

"Half-covered in soot and reeking of the fire that had almost consumed it, a corner of the quilt survived, its **luminous** triangles still triumphantly marching."

Synonyms

EXERCISE 8 Use the Thesaurus

Explain how the meaning of the phrase changes with the use of each synonym.

"Clara, who helped my mother, was ***gingerly*** *dusting the curio cabinet with a feather duster* one afternoon when she knocked over a cup and broke off its handle."

1. *gingerly* ______________________________
2. *timidly* ______________________________
3. *guardedly* ______________________________
4. *delicately* ______________________________

Compound Sentences

What is a compound sentence?

A compound sentence is two or more simple sentences of equal importance joined together either with a coordinating conjunction, a semicolon, or an adverbial conjunction.

Notice how the following two sentences can be joined to make one compound sentence using three methods.

The collection of dainty cups came to me. I gave them a place of honor in my first home.

Method 1

Use a coordinating conjunction with a comma before it to join two sentences.

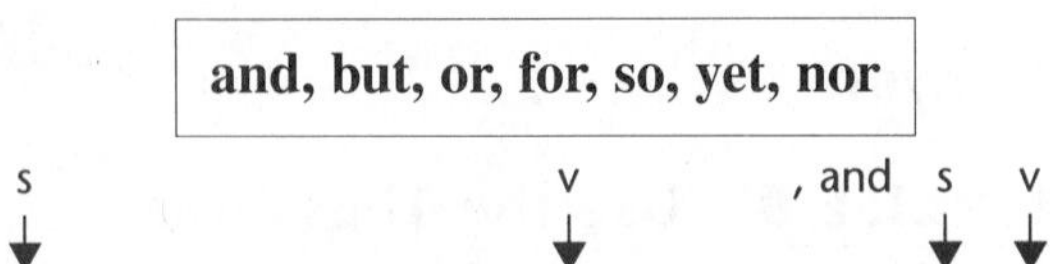

The collection of dainty cups came to me, ***and*** I gave them a place of honor in my first home.

Method 2

Use a semicolon to join two sentences that are closely related in ideas.

The collection of dainty cups came to me**;** I gave them a place of honor in my home.

Method 3

Use a transition word after the semicolon to show a relationship between the two sentences. These transition words are called adverbial conjunctions.

then, however, consequently, however, otherwise, nevertheless, nonetheless, on the other hand

Notice that a comma is added after the adverbial conjunction to separate the word from the next sentence.

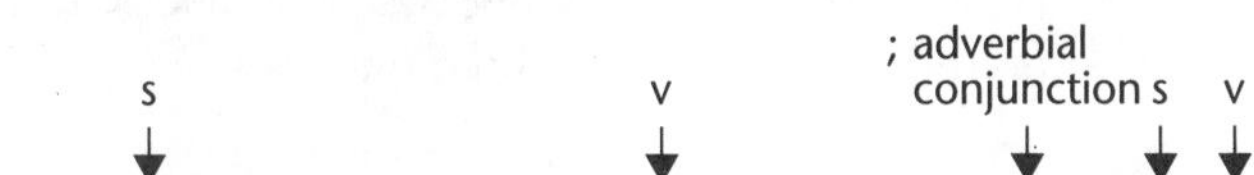

The collection of dainty cups came to me**;** ***therefore,*** I gave them a place of honor in my home.

EXERCISE 9 Write Compound Sentences

Write each simple sentence as a compound sentence by joining to it another simple sentence. Use what is indicated in the parentheses. Add punctuation as needed.

EXAMPLE

My immigrant parents paid off their debts. (yet)

My immigrant parents paid off their debts**, yet** they always felt poor.

1. I heard the crash. (so)

____

____

2. Hard times were with us for many months. (however)

____

____

3. We drove to the farm. (then)

____

____

4. Her words came back to me. (;)

____

____

5. No one could touch the fragile dishes. (therefore)

____

____

6. The lesson is significant. (yet)

____

____

7. I was reading nearby. (and)

____

____

8. Clara helped my mother. (;)

____

____

9. A delivery van replaced our lumpy couch. (so)

____

____

10. I worked in another part of the house. (consequently)

____

____

Sentence Style

EXERCISE 10 Rearrange Sentences

Rewrite each sentence using the indicated new beginning. Be sure to keep the meaning of the original sentence. Consider the effect of rearranging the words.

1. My immigrant parents paid off debts, rebuilding financial security dollar by dollar.

   By paying off debts, ______________________________

   ____

   ____

2. Clara was gingerly dusting the curio cabinet with a feather duster one afternoon when she knocked over a cup and broke off its handle.

   Gingerly dusting ______________________________________

   ____

   ____

3. One winter morning while I worked in another part of the house, my daughter climbed on a chair to reach the cups.

   While I was ______________________________________

   ____

   ____

4. My husband and I drove to the farm the day after the fire, grateful to find much of the house still standing.

   My husband and I were grateful ______________________________

   ____

   ____

EXERCISE 11 Combine Sentences

Combine the ideas from the sentences in each group to write one new sentence. As you write each sentence, consider the emphasis and relationships you want to achieve.

1.

My mother had a collection of small English bone china cups.

The cups were gold-rimmed.

These cups were inside the cabinet.

____

____

____

2.

She carried the two fragments of china.

She was crying.

She took the fragments to my mother.

____

____

____

3.

Sometimes I would take the cups down.

I took them down one by one.

I showed them to my daughter.

____

____

____

4.

I hugged the quilt to my breast.

I carried it into the sunshine.

I spread it on the grass.

____

____

____

Revising the Essay

EXERCISE 12 Rework for Content, Structure, Language, and Accuracy

Part A

Reread the body paragraphs of your essay. Does each paragraph address the needs for factual readers? Imaginative readers? Curious readers? Revise your paragraphs by adding additional details. Would focused readers want anything omitted? If so, omit these details.

Part B

Locate at least two adjacent simple sentences that could be improved by combining them into a compound sentence. Highlight these two sentences. Write the revised sentences at the bottom of the page.

Part C

Proofread your paper to correct misspelled words, typographical errors, and missing words. Using the revisions you made on your draft, write a final copy of your essay.

CHAPTER 6

Traditions

Traditions: Exploring the Theme

You may have heard the term "the cycle of years." A year is itself a cycle; spring turns to summer, summer turns to fall, fall turns to winter. Each year you have the opportunity to live through the cycle another time. As you repeat the process of celebrating annual events and holidays, certain people, foods, decorations, and activities become important to you. In this way, traditions develop to be repeated in much the same way year after year. The author of this selection tells about passing on traditions important to her and her family.

EXERCISE 1 Prepare to Read

1. Why do people have traditions?

____

____

2. What are some typically American traditions?

____

____

The Torch by Laura B. Randolph

ABOUT THE AUTHOR

A native of Washington, D.C., Laura B. Randolph is an honor graduate of Georgetown Law Center. An author of numerous articles on national affairs, Randolph was named White House correspondent during the Clinton administration. She has coauthored several books with entertainer Patti Labelle. As senior editor for *Ebony* magazine, Randolph has shared her views on issues of human interest including marriage, mothers, abuse, and black women in Congress.

---

1 I have two indelible[1] memories of the first and only time I cooked the family Thanksgiving dinner. One is how truly awful the food tasted—the

[1] **indelible** permanent, unforgettable

turkey was dry, the string beans irreparably[2] mushy, and the pumpkin pies store bought. The other is of how my mother, along with all the other family elders, pretended not to notice.

2 If you knew my mother, and the other over-fifty folks to whom I am related, you would know how significant this is. As a rule, they have no pity on the rest of us. They come from the old school that says the only way a daughter/son/niece/nephew will learn to do something right is to be told when and how he or she has done it wrong.

3 So, last year, when they all sat down to dinner and not one of them so much as mentioned the paper plates, the mismatched stemware, and the everyday silver, I was certain their collective shock had rendered them speechless. When my mother—the family matriarch, the woman who has never set a holiday table that didn't come straight out of the pages of *House Beautiful:* exquisite china, a white linen tablecloth, sterling flatware polished to a gleam that very morning—surveyed the table and pronounced it "lovely," I wasn't just baffled, I was chilled to the bone.

4 It didn't stop there. Calmly, coolly, as if she were saying, "Please pass the gravy," my mother turned to my only male cousin, Tony, and asked him to carve the turkey. A hush fell over the table. No one moved. Ignoring the paper plates is one thing. If my family has one sacred Thanksgiving tradition, however, it is that my uncle, Tony's father, carves the bird. It is a task he always performs with great fanfare and anticipation and has never entrusted to anyone, not even the year his carving hand was in a cast because he'd cut his finger off with a saw. "Great idea," my uncle said to my mother, as he passed his son the knife.

5 Who were these people? What had they done with my real family? What was happening here? A rite[3] of passage. That, I later came to realize, was the only explanation. That Thanksgiving, something was being passed on—from mother to daughter, from father to son, from one generation to the next. It was the reason behind my mother's sudden and inexplicable[4] announcement that she would no longer be preparing our traditional Thanksgiving feast. Now I see her decision was never about who cooked the bird. It was about pushing us from the nest.

6 My family elders, the keepers of our heritage, had deemed the time right to begin passing on the family legacy.[5] They had decided it was time to tell us, their sons and daughters, that one day soon the responsibility of gathering the family together, of keeping it close, would be ours. When my uncle passed his son the knife, he really was passing the torch and sending us all a message: The clock was ticking. Soon, it would be up to us to preserve

[2] **irreparably** not able to be repaired or improved [3] **rite** ceremony, ritual

[4] **inexplicable** not able to be explained, mysterious

[5] **legacy** gift, inheritance

the family traditions—my father's oyster casserole, my aunts' cobblers, my uncle's skill with a knife—that have connected one generation to the next and, most important, provided the essential roots and rhythms of our lives. And, in this way, we are talking about so much more than Thanksgiving and place settings and turkeys. We're talking about traditions that have been passed on for thousands of years, in one form or another, updated and imprinted by each generation before being passed on to the next.

7 Something of our ancestors' teachings still lives on in each of us. If we continue to foster[6] them, these teachings will live forever, with a unifying force, a quiet power, that has taught us how to survive and flourish in a hostile world—how to seize new opportunities and make the most of whatever difficult situations we may face. That, my family elders knew, was the real value of the traditions they were passing on. Thanksgiving was only the beginning. With each passing year we, the next generation, will be charged with more and more responsibility so that we can move forward knowing what it takes to raise our own families.

8 Now, as this Thanksgiving approaches, I have come to understand that my family members know their children intimately. Each of them knows that, if the transition were to be successful, the torch had to be passed slowly, carefully. Otherwise, when the day came when we, their children, were the elders, we wouldn't know how to keep it lit or burning. And if the passage were too swift or too sudden, we might find it too hot—or too heavy—to hold.

9 It begins with Thanksgiving. At least it can. For me, that is no easy challenge. I have never felt at home in the kitchen, and my mother knows this. Until recently, the only thing I have ever made for dinner with any skill or flair is reservations. Unlike my mother's culinary skill, my style of cooking can best be described as new wave. Better still, microwave. Fast food. Blink of the eye. Push of the button. Until now, culinary skill was never important to me. Until now, however, I never understood that when my mother was in the kitchen, she wasn't just making our dinner, she was making our memories; she wasn't just blending spices, she was blending generations.

10 Weeks before the holiday, I stood in her kitchen stirring and seasoning.

11 "Take your time," my mother told me, showing me how to baste the turkey and knead the bread.

12 "Time isn't the answer," I said, stomping my foot the way I did when I was a child. No matter how many times I do it, I told her, it doesn't taste like hers.

13 "That's what I used to say to your grandmother," my mother said, tying her apron around me.

[6] **foster** nurture, take care of

EXERCISE 2 Reflect on What You Have Read

Finding Facts

1. What traditional activity is "the torch" that Uncle Tony passes to his son?

___

Making Inferences

2. Why don't the older relatives make mention of the paper plates, mismatched stemware, and everyday silver? ___

___

___

Sharing Reactions

3. What do you learn about the author from what she has written? Explain.

___

___

___

FOCUSING ON The Illustrative Essay

An illustrative essay, developed with illustrations and examples, is one of the most commonly used types of writing in academics. For instance, you may be asked: to give examples of cultures in sociology, to illustrate the circulatory system in biology, or to exemplify types of investments in a business class. Regardless of the assignment, the body of the illustrative essay requires solid examples to help the reader see your points.

An illustrative essay, like any essay, needs well-constructed introductory and concluding paragraphs to provide direction for readers.

The introduction or the first paragraph of an essay has the powerful function of laying the groundwork for what is to come in the body of the essay. This first paragraph must engage the reader's attention, provide some background for the topic, and, in general, lead up to the main point or thesis of the essay. Because of its purpose, an introductory paragraph has a unique structure.

Introductory Paragraph

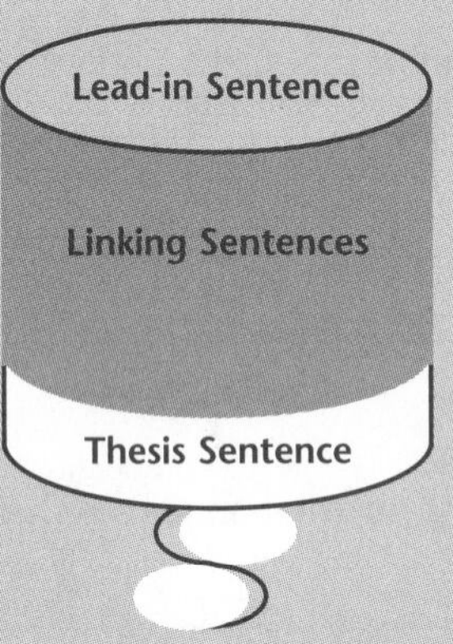

An introductory paragraph has three sections: the lead-in sentence, the link, and the thesis sentence. In contrast to a typical body paragraph where the main idea or topic sentence is stated first, an introductory paragraph builds to the thesis of the essay, which is written as the last sentence.

What is a lead-in sentence?

The first sentence of the introduction, appropriately called a **lead-in sentence,** introduces your topic and encourages the reader to become involved in what you have to say.

There is a variety of techniques for writing the opening sentence. Following are eight different approaches with examples of each based on the thesis, ***"I want to build traditions that have meaning for my family."*** Any one of the following techniques could be used as the first sentence of an introductory paragraph.

TECHNIQUES FOR WRITING LEAD-IN SENTENCES

Technique	Example of Lead-in Sentence
Start with a general statement about your thesis or with a definition.	*A family is a community of people who share traditions.*
Use a main word from the thesis as a starting point to hook the attention of the reader.	*I wish my parents had been more involved with family traditions.*

Provide some historical background.	*I can remember vividly the times our family used to spend with my grandparents before they passed away.*
Start with a quotation.	*"It is a wise father that knows his own child," said Shakespeare more than four hundred years ago.*
Ask a question.	*What makes a father a "dad"?*
Tell a story.	*As a little boy, I used to watch television, pretending that a dad on one of the shows was my dad.*
Start with a statement of an opposite position.	*I grew up with parents focused on earning a decent living and generally concerned about my well-being.*
State the importance of the topic.	*Without traditions, a family is little more than a group of people living in the same place.*

What are linking sentences?

LEAD-IN SENTENCE
↓
LINKING SENTENCES
↓
THESIS SENTENCE

After you have decided on an opening sentence for the introductory paragraph, you "link" the lead-in sentence and the thesis. One or more transition sentences lead the reader logically from the opening idea to the thesis.

Where is the thesis sentence located?

The **thesis sentence** is the final sentence of the introductory paragraph. After attracting your readers' attention with your opening sentence, lead your readers to your main point, stated in the thesis sentence, and then on to the body paragraphs.

Examples of Introductory Paragraphs

1. *Start with a general statement about your thesis or with a definition.*

   (LEAD-IN) *A family is a community of people who share traditions.* **(LINK)** In my family when I was growing up, there were my mother, my father, my brother and me. I can't say that we had many traditions, however, that made us a real family. On Thanksgiving Day, for example, we went to the grocery store to buy our complete turkey dinner, already cooked, wrapped in aluminum packets. **(THESIS)** Now that I'm a parent with a two-year-old son, I want to build traditions that have meaning for my family.

2. *Use a main word from the thesis as a starting point to hook the attention of the reader.*

   (LEAD-IN) *I wish my parents had been more involved with family traditions.* **(LINK)** When I was growing up, Mom and Dad were so busy with other things that they didn't focus on meaningful traditions but did things the easy way. On Thanksgiving Day, for example, we went to the grocery store to buy our complete turkey dinner, already cooked, wrapped in aluminum packets. **(THESIS)** Now that I'm a parent with a two-year-old son, I want to build traditions that have meaning for my family.

3. *Provide some historical background.*

   (LEAD-IN) *I can remember vividly the times our family used to spend with my grandparents before they passed away.* **(LINK)** With their deaths, we lost the family traditions that had been important to us. No longer did the whole family get together for the holidays. On Thanksgiving Day, instead, Mom went to the grocery store to buy the three of us a complete turkey dinner, already cooked, wrapped in aluminum packets. **(THESIS)** Now that I'm a parent with a two-year-old son, I want to build traditions that have meaning for my family.

4. *Start with a quotation.*

   (LEAD-IN) *"It is a wise father that knows his own child," Shakespeare stated more than four hundred years ago.* **(LINK)** My own father wasn't wise enough to know that family traditions were important to me. For instance, I was not happy that on Thanksgiving Day we went to the grocery store to buy a complete turkey dinner, already cooked, wrapped in aluminum packets. Perhaps I can be a wise father myself and give my family something I didn't have. **(THESIS)** Now that I'm a parent with a two-year-old son, I want to build traditions that have meaning for my family.

5. *Ask a question.*

   (LEAD-IN) *What makes a father a dad?* **(LINK)** A dad is a father who makes a family for his children. My own father didn't truly value family, and he didn't build meaningful family traditions for us kids. On Thanksgiving Day, for example, we simply went to the grocery store to buy a complete turkey dinner, already cooked, wrapped in aluminum packets. I want to be a dad, not just a father, and give my family something I didn't have. **(THESIS)** Now that I'm a parent with a two-year-old son, I want to build traditions that have meaning for my family.

6. *Tell a story.*

   (LEAD-IN) *As a little boy, I used to watch television, pretending that a dad on one of the shows was my dad.* **(LINK)** My TV dad would know how important family traditions were to me. He would not go to the grocery store on Thanksgiving Day to buy a complete turkey dinner, already cooked, wrapped in aluminum packets. My TV dad wasn't my real parent, however, and I was left disappointed by our lack of family spirit. **(THESIS)** Now that I'm a parent with a two-year-old son, I want to build traditions that have meaning for us as a family.

7. *Start with a statement of an opposite position.*

   (LEAD-IN) *I grew up with parents focused on earning a decent living and generally concerned about my well being.* **(LINK)** They were, however, apathetic to establishing any family tradition. On Thanksgiving Day, for example, we went to the grocery store to buy our complete turkey dinner, already cooked, wrapped in aluminum packets. **(THESIS)** Now that I'm a parent with a two-year-old son, I want to build traditions that have meaning for my family.

8. *State the importance of the topic.*

   (LEAD-IN) *Without traditions, a family is little more than a group of people living in the same place.* **(LINK)** My mother, father, brother, and I lived in the same house, but we weren't a true family. We didn't celebrate meaningful traditions together. On Thanksgiving Day, for example, we simply went to the grocery store to buy a complete turkey dinner, already cooked, wrapped in aluminum packets. Today as an adult, perhaps I can do my part to turn the group of people who live with me into a true family. **(THESIS)** Now that I'm a parent with a two-year-old son, I want to build traditions that have meaning for my family.

Concluding Paragraph

A public speaker of note says that in giving a speech, you should simply

Tell them what you are going to tell them.

Tell them.

Tell them what you told them.

Similarly, in writing an essay, the introductory paragraph tells what you are going to write about. Then, the body paragraphs tell the important information. The final paragraph, or the conclusion of the essay, tells what you have just told about.

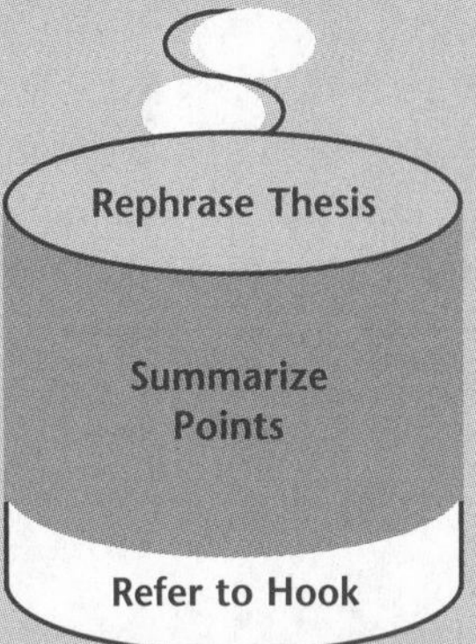

The concludion of an essay has the purpose of satisfying readers that you have accomplished your goal. You can order a conclusion as a reverse of an introduction. That is, you start the conclusion with a reminder of your thesis, then summarize briefly your main points, and finally, in your last sentence, make a reference to the idea you used as a lead-in sentence. This technique brings your writing full circle in a way that is complete and satisfying.

Building from example introductory paragraph #5, a writer could conclude the essay about traditions as follows.

> **(RESTATEMENT OF THESIS)** Eating dinners with my son, spending time together, and helping with homework—these are the traditions I want to develop as Jason grows. **(BRIEF SUMMARY)** These rituals will allow us to build a solid family and keep close to each other over the years. **(REFERENCE TO LEAD-IN SENTENCE)** My parents were satisfied simply when my physical needs were met, but for me, I know there is more to being a father.

Developing an Essay

Assignment 6: Writing about Tradition

Laura B. Randolph writes about Thanksgiving, a yearly event celebrated in her family. She shows that the responsibility for carrying on this tradition is being passed from one generation to the next. Although the Thanksgiving meal she prepares does not match the ones prepared by her mother, Randolph comes to realize her role in preserving family tradition, a role that she will become increasingly comfortable in as time goes by.

The word *tradition* means "the passing down of elements of culture from one generation to the next" or "a time-honored practice." Many families have a variety of traditions that are important to them from one generation to the next. These traditions may center on religious or national holidays. They may be related to birthdays, anniversaries, or reunions. Some relatives have a time-honored practice of going together to find bargains at "back-to-school" or mid-winter sales. You may be a part of a family that celebrates in creative ways. Some families spend time together one night of each week with snacks and conversation. In certain families, members wouldn't miss getting together for the first day of the hunting season or the last of the berry picking season.

Often, it is friends who have time-honored practices. Some people gather each year at a special sporting event or around the TV for the Super Bowl. Groups schedule regular lunches or dinners together to keep in touch, maybe in someone's home or in a favorite eatery. Some friends traditionally exchange gifts for important occasions. You may be part of a group that gets together regularly to play cards, dance, or watch movies.

School groups have traditions. Perhaps your school has a moving-up-day ceremony. Maybe a sports team has a ritual for preparing for away games or for the big game of the season. Even coworkers have traditions: eating bagels on Monday morning or decorating the office of someone who has earned a promotion. Some individuals have their own traditions that might be as simple as walking through the park each spring to see the early crocuses or doing the crossword puzzle in Sunday's newspaper.

For Writing Assignment 6, write an essay telling about a tradition or traditions that you practice, that you would like to establish, or that you would like to change or eliminate.

The Writing Process

Looping

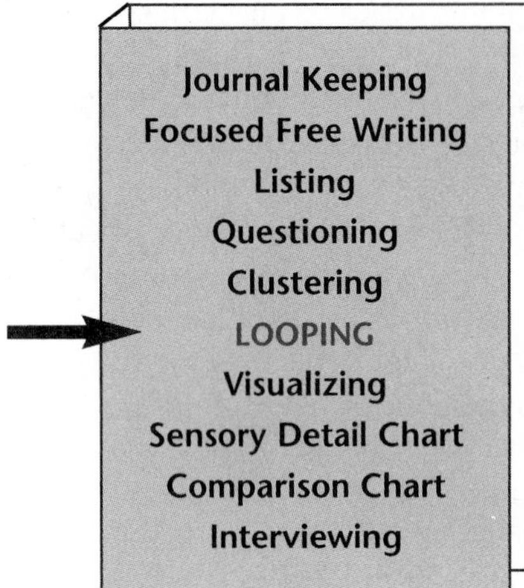

Looping is quite similar to focused free writing. Write your topic on the top of a page and free write about this topic for several minutes; let one idea flow into the next. Reread your free writing to find a phrase or sentence that interests you.

Copy these words on the top of a new page; write about these words for several minutes. Once again, find and copy key words. Continue this looping until you have generated enough ideas to organize a paper.

Read an abbreviated example of looping.

Page 1

Tradition. What traditions do I have? Every year we celebrate Easter, Thanksgiving, and Christmas. When Grandpa was alive we got dressed up for the holidays. Now it's more relaxed; Grandma still tries hard to keep the family traditions. She's a great cook. She only eats out at restaurants when we take her. Grandpa liked only Grandma's pasta sauce. She cooked for hours every Sunday. You knew it was Sunday just by the smell. There was one sauce I hated. I couldn't stand the smell of calamari. Grandpa loved it, so Grandma made it for him every Christmas. She served it over homemade noodles. She used to make the dough early in the morning so it would be fresh, and then she cranked out the noodles on an old machine from Italy. Sometimes I helped her turn the handle and watched the noodles ooze out in long strips.

Page 2

I can't stand the smell of calamari. Calamari is supposed to be a specialty, but no one in the family besides Grandma and Grandpa really liked it. Grandma kept cooking it for Christmas even after Grandpa died. No one had the heart to tell her how much we disliked it. One time she asked me to help her clean the squid, and I thought I would puke. Thank heavens she didn't serve calamari on Thanksgiving. Thanksgiving was different. We had turkey with two types of dressing, homemade lasagna, and a ham. While the women cooked in the kitchen, the men gathered in the living room watching television. Then, Uncle Dominick bought Grandma another television for her bedroom. The next Thanksgiving, Uncle Dominick brought the second television downstairs because Uncle Sal and he couldn't agree on what game to watch. I liked playing with my younger cousins. If it wasn't too cold outside, we'd go out on our bikes in front of the house.

Page 3

The next Thanksgiving, Uncle Dominick brought the second television downstairs because Uncle Sal and he couldn't agree on what game to watch. All we ever heard were the sounds of the televisions blasting and our uncles shouting and arguing about which team was better and who made the better play. The only time they shut the television off was when Grandma called everyone into the dining room for dinner. Then we had fun—everyone talking at once, sampling all the food. I'd be so stuffed, I could hardly move from the table. After a while, Grandma would make a toast to Grandpa, and we'd all get quiet remembering him. I remember when I went to his funeral. I was a teenager then. But, when I was younger I remember going to my Aunt Louise's funeral. It was winter, and everybody was dressed in black. Grandpa had to hold Grandma up because she kept crumpling. I can remember looking at Aunt Louise and never being so scared in my life.

Page 4

I remember going to my Aunt Louise's funeral. Even though it's been twenty years, I can still remember my terror. There's no way I'll ever make my kids go to a funeral unless they're old enough to handle it.

Well, I guess I had a lot of traditions that I liked growing up, but I think I'll write about some things I want to change.

An Essay Plan

Read an outline plan based on the looping.

Title Snuffing Out Unwelcome Traditions

Thesis Three of my family traditions, in particular, I loathe and intend to transform.

I. Topic sentence for first body paragraph	I. Children should be mature enough to attend a funeral.
A. Major point	A. my terrible experience
B. Major point	B. a change
II. Topic sentence for second body paragraph	II. During Thanksgiving, only one television should be tuned to football.
A. Major point	A. too noisy
B. Major point	B. new rule
III. Topic sentence for third body paragraph	III. For Christmas, a dish besides calamari sauce should be served.
A. Major point	A. reaction to calamari sauce
B. Major point	B. another sauce

A Model Essay

SNUFFING OUT UNWANTED TRADITIONS

1 For years members of my large family have quietly endured practices firmly entrenched as time-honored traditions. After suffering through these traditions for too long, I have decided my mission is to douse these unwelcome traditions now, swiftly and totally. Like the Knight of the Crusades, I will show no mercy on anyone or anything that stands in my way. Three of my family traditions, in particular, I loathe and intend to transform.

2 First and foremost, the tradition of requiring children to attend funerals (a "showing" as my relatives call them), when a child is neither mentally nor emotionally ready, is dreadful. I remember vividly how terrorized I felt at my first showing. I was six years old. When I first saw the corpse, I thought it was going to jump out of the casket and come running after me. I absolutely refused to let go of my father's hand and clung to him desperately. As my relatives sobbed in anguish around me, I felt queasy to the point of nearly vomiting. Today, as a parent of three children, ages eleven, nine, and seven, I will not take them to a showing until I think they're emotionally ready to handle it. I know that several of my cousins agree.

3 The next tradition I will tackle—zoning the televisions to football on Thanksgiving Day—is more daunting because of the opposition I know I will encounter. At my grandmother's house, where the family traditionally gathers on Thanksgiving, there are two televisions, and both are tuned to football. From the kitchen and living room, we hear obnoxious yelling coming from the two separate groups of hyped-up viewers. The football fans in my family can never agree on which game to watch, so someone grabs the remote control to go channel surfing. Inevitably, we end up with each set on a different game. The rest of the family suffers in silence because there's no place in the house where anybody can go to get away from the shouts and insults. I think if I work with some of my cousins, my aunts, and even my grandmother beforehand, we can salvage at least one TV for the rest of us and leave the die-hard football fans to figure out which game they will watch.

4 Finally, every Christmas my grandmother prepares calamari (squid) sauce to blanket fresh pasta. Out of respect for my grandmother, the majority of my family pretends to like the fishy-tasting, rubbery-textured, and awful-smelling seafood. As the dish gets passed around the huge dining room table, my grandmother

eagerly watches as we take some sauce for the pasta. As artfully as I can, I try to disguise my revulsion for squid by moving the sauce to a corner of my plate. When it comes time to clear the table, we always insist that grandma sit and relax after all her time preparing in the kitchen, so we can quickly dispose of the detested calamari. This year I will encourage my grandmother to prepare, in addition to the calamari, a pot of her homemade Italian sausage and meatball pasta sauce so we can choose which of her two "great" sauces we want to eat.

5 With my perseverance and the support of other family members, certain traditions in my family will be altered. Funerals will be attended by self-choice, only one television will be tuned to football during Thanksgiving, and another sauce will be served along with the "dreaded calamari" on Christmas. I am determined to accomplish these tasks, and I am hopeful that by the end of this year, these new traditions will snuff out the existing ones and will be carried on for generations to come.

EXERCISE 3 React to the Illustrative Essay

Answer the following questions to show your understanding of thesis, order of development, and introductory paragraph.

1. What technique does the writer use as an opening sentence? (Refer to Techniques for Writing Lead-in Sentences.) ____________________

____

____

2. What details does the writer provide for factual, imaginative, and curious readers?

____

____

____

____

Work on Writing Assignment 6

EXERCISE 4 Prewrite, Plan, and Draft

Part A

On separate paper, use looping to prewrite.

Part B

Using the ideas you gather by looping, complete a plan for your essay.

Title ____

Thesis sentence (essay map) ____

____

____

Underline **key words** in your thesis.

Controlling question ____

Topic Sentence # 1 ____

(Circle synonyms that link the topic sentence to your thesis sentence.)

a. ____

b. ____

c. ____

Topic Sentence # 2 ____

(Circle synonyms that link the topic sentence to your thesis sentence.)

a. ____

b. ______________________________

c. ______________________________

Topic Sentence # 3 ______________________________

(Circle synonyms that link the topic sentence to your thesis sentence.)

a. ______________________________

b. ______________________________

c. ______________________________

Part C

1. Write an introductory paragraph based on the thesis you wrote in Part B.

____

____

____

____

____

____

2. Using the same thesis, write another introductory paragraph using a different lead-in sentence. ______________________________

____

____

____

____

____

3. Using the introduction you prefer, write a draft of your essay.

Building Language Skills

Vocabulary

EXERCISE 5 Use the Dictionary

Write dictionary definitions of the word *render.*

____

____

____

____

____

____

Underline the definition of the word as it is used in the sentence.

> "So, last year, when they all sat down to dinner and not one of them so much as mentioned the paper plates, the mismatched stemware, and the everyday silver, I was certain their collective shock had ***rendered*** them speechless."

EXERCISE 6 Use the Thesaurus

Explain how the meaning of the phrase changes with the use of each synonym.

> "If my family has one ***sacred*** Thanksgiving tradition, however, it is that my uncle, Tony's father, carves the bird."

1. one ***sacred*** Thanksgiving tradition ______________________
2. one ***revered*** Thanksgiving tradition ______________________
3. one ***special*** Thanksgiving tradition ______________________
4. one ***respected*** Thanksgiving tradition ______________________

Complex Sentences

Which one of the two sentences appears to be more complex?

1. My family elders, the keepers of our heritage, had deemed the time right to begin passing on the family legacy.

or

2. When we sat down for dinner, no one mentioned the paper plates.

In common usage, the word *complex* means *complicated*, or *involved*, so the first sentence is the more complex one. Grammatically, the word *complex*, however, has a specialized meaning. Although sentence #1 may be longer and more complex in idea, it is grammatically a simple sentence. The second, shorter sentence #2 is grammatically complex.

What is a complex sentence?

A **complex sentence** is one that contains an independent clause and one or more dependent clauses. A **dependent clause** is a group of words that has a subject and a verb but cannot stand alone as a sentence.

The words in the list that follows are signals for dependent clauses. If one of these words is followed by a subject and verb, the group of words is a dependent clause.

after	than	whereas
although	that	whether
as (as if)	though	while
because	unless	which
before	until	who
how	what	whom
if	when	whose
since	where	why

Notice how the italicized dependent clauses in the following complex sentences explain relationships.

> *When my family sat down to dinner,* not one of them mentioned the paper plates, the mismatched stemware, and the everyday silver.

> My family has a sacred Thanksgiving tradition, *that my uncle carves the bird.*

EXERCISE 7 Write Compound and Complex Sentences

Next to each number indicate whether the sentence is simple (S), compound (C), or complex (Cx). If a sentence is compound, rewrite it as a complex sentence.

_____ 1. My mother turned to my only male cousin, and she asked him to carve the turkey.

____

____

____

_____ 2. When my uncle passed his son the knife, he was really passing the torch.

____

____

____

_____ 3 I have never felt at home in the kitchen, and my mother knows my feeling.

____

____

____

_____ 4. If we continue to foster these teachings, they will live forever.

____

____

____

_____ 5. Weeks before the holiday, I stood in her kitchen stirring and seasoning.

____

____

____

______ 6. A hush fell over the table, and no one moved.

____

____

____

Sentence Style

EXERCISE 8 Rearrange Sentences

Rewrite each sentence using the indicated new beginning. Be sure to keep the meaning of the original sentence. Consider the effect of rearranging the words.

1. My mother turned to my cousin and asked him to carve the turkey.

   When, ______________________________________

   ____

   ____

   ____

2. Something of our ancestors' teachings still lives on in each of us.

   Living on in each of us ______________________________________

   ____

   ____

   ____

3. If the passage were too swift or too sudden, we might find the torch too hot—or too heavy—to hold.

   We might find the torch ______________________________________

   ____

4. If you knew my mother, you would know how significant her reaction was.

To know ____

EXERCISE 9 Combine Sentences

Combine the ideas from the sentences in each group to write one new sentence. As you write each sentence, consider the emphasis and relationships you want to achieve.

1.

Once I cooked the Thanksgiving dinner.

The Thanksgiving dinner began the passing on of our family legacy.

2.

Last year the family sat down to dinner.

Not one of them so much as mentioned the paper plates.

No one mentioned the mismatched stemware.

No one mentioned the everyday silver.

3.

My family has one sacred Thanksgiving tradition.

It involves my Uncle Tony.

My uncle is the one who carves the bird.

____

____

____

4.

My mother was in the kitchen.

She wasn't just making our dinner.

She was making our memories.

____

____

____

Revising The Essay

EXERCISE 10 Rework for Content, Structure, Language, and Accuracy

Part A

1. Label each part of your introductory paragraph—lead-in sentence, linking sentences, thesis sentence.
2. Label each part of your concluding paragraph—restated thesis, brief summary, reference to lead-in sentence.
3. Read to make sure you have answered your controlling question.

Part B

1. Circle two different words that can be made more precise. Write in the margin, near each circled word, the new word. Decide whether to use the original word or its synonym.

2. Highlight at least one complex sentence in your essay. If your essay does not include a complex sentence, write one.
3. Highlight at least one sentence that can be enhanced by rearranging the words. Rewrite the new sentence at the bottom of your paper.

Part C

Using the changes you made in your draft, type a final copy of your essay. Proofread your paper to correct misspelled words, typographical errors, and missing words.

CHAPTER 7

Education

Education: Exploring the Theme

Education can take place under unexpected circumstances and in unpredictable ways. Schools, however, provide a conventional source of important learning opportunities for people of all ages, and a skilled and caring professional teacher can make a difference in a student's life. The author of this selection reminisces about learning something of value from one of his high school teachers.

EXERCISE 1 Prepare to Read

1. What is education?

 ____

 ____

2. What value do people put on education today?

 ____

 ____

From *Breaking Barriers: A Memoir* by Carl Rowan

ABOUT THE AUTHOR

Breaking Barriers: A Memoir by Carl Rowan tells a story of racial change in America from an insider's perspective. In this selection from his book, Rowan provides a glimpse of himself as a high school student in a poverty-stricken area in Tennessee. Rowan went on to serve as a naval officer, a reporter, and an award-winning columnist. A spokesperson for the disadvantaged, he worked with Martin Luther King Jr. and other activists in support of civil rights.

---

1 It was so difficult in those depression years to focus on much other than getting enough to eat, and girls, and whupping Lynchburg or Gallatin on the gridiron. I shall be forever grateful that one marvelous teacher forced me to focus on some other things.

2 She was only an inch or so above five feet tall and probably never weighed more than 110 pounds in her eighty-five years, but she was the only woman tough enough to make me read *Beowulf* and think for a few foolish days that I liked it. I refer to Miss Bessie—Mrs. Bessie Taylor Gwynn—

the woman who taught me English, literature, history, civics, and a lot more than I realized when I attended Bernard High from 1938 to 1942.

3 I shall never forget the day she scolded me, insisting that I wasn't reading enough of the things she wanted me to read.

4 "But, Miss Bessie," I complained, "I ain't much interested in *Beowulf.*" She fastened on me her large brown eyes that became daggerish[1] slits and said, "Boy, I am your *English* teacher, and I know I've taught you better than this. How dare you talk to me with 'I ain't' this and 'I ain't' that?"

5 "Miss Bessie," I said, "I'm trying to make first-string end on the football team. If I go around saying 'it isn't' and 'they aren't,' the guys are gonna laugh me off the squad."

6 "Boy," she said, "you'll make first string only because you have guts and can play football. But do you know what *really* takes guts? Refusing to lower your standards to those of the dumb crowd. It takes guts to say to yourself that you've got to live and be somebody fifty years after these football games are over." I started saying "we aren't" and "if I were," and I still made first-string left end and class valedictorian[2] without losing the respect of my buddies. I remembered that with a special sense of tragedy when I read recently that many black kids were afraid to display knowledge or scholarship for fear that their peers would accuse them of acting white.

7 Miss Bessie died in 1980 after a remarkable forty-seven years in which she taught my mother, me, my brother and sisters, and hundreds of other black youngsters who were deprived economically, in terms of family backgrounds, and in almost every other measurement of disadvantage. She would be *unforgettable* to most of her pupils under any circumstance. I remember her with special gratitude and affection in this era when Americans are so wrought up about a "rising tide of mediocrity"[3] in public education. They worry about finding competent, caring teachers to help their children to cope in an increasingly technological, sophisticated, and dangerous world.

8 Mrs. Gwynn was an example of an aphorism[4] we must accept: An informed, dedicated teacher is a blessing to children and an asset to the nation not even remotely reflected in what most of our teachers are paid. Miss Bessie had a bearing of dignity—an unpretentious[5] pride that told anyone who met her she was educated in the best sense of that word.

[1] **daggerish** like daggers

[2] **valedictorian** graduating senior with the highest grades

[3] **mediocrity** ordinariness, commonness

[4] **aphorism** motto, slogan

[5] **unpretentious** modest, humble, unassuming

There was never a discipline problem in her classes. We knew instinctively that you didn't mess around with a woman who knew all about the Battle of Hastings, the Magna Carta and Runnymede, the Bill of Rights, the Kellogg-Briand Pact outlawing war, the Emancipation Proclamation—and could also play the piano.

9 This frail-looking woman, who could make sense of the writings of Shakespeare, Milton, Voltaire, and bring to life Booker T. Washington and W. E. B. Du Bois, was a towering presence in our classrooms. We students memorized the names of members of the Supreme Court and the President's Cabinet, having learned early that it could be very embarrassing to be unprepared when Miss Bessie said, "Get up and tell the class who Frances Perkins is and what you know and think about her."

10 I wonder how many teachers today make their students learn the names of officials who spend the public's money and make policies that affect us all so profoundly.

EXERCISE 2 Reflect on What You Have Read

Finding Facts

1. What was Miss Bessie's musical talent?

____

Making Inferences

2. How did Miss Bessie's students react to her when she was their teacher?

____

____

Sharing Reactions

3. What is Miss Bessie's philosophy of education? Do you agree with her? Why? Why not?

____

____

____

FOCUSING ON The Narrative Essay

A narrative essay is one that tells a story, or even several stories, to explain or prove a point. Most readers relate well to a narrative essay since they enjoy knowing what happens to somebody else and can apply the story to their own experience. Many important points can be made through storytelling. Important considerations in a narrative are the sequence of events, the characterization, and the setting.

Sequence

A narrative essay follows a logical time sequence. Events are usually arranged in a straightforward, chronological way. In *Breaking Barriers: A Memoir,* Carl Rowan tells what happened from the beginning of the story to the end. Writers sometimes use an order other than straightforward, chronological order to engage the reader's interest. If the middle or end of a story is more captivating than the beginning, you may begin at one of these points and move backward to finish the story. You may have seen this technique, called "flashback," used in movies.

You can fit a narrative into the framework of your essay. The introductory paragraph provides background for your story and the thesis or main idea. The body paragraphs develop the narrative, and the concluding paragraph reminds your reader of the point that the story made.

Rowan writes this conclusion: "I wonder how many teachers today make their students learn the names of officials who spend the public's money and make policies that affect us all so profoundly." He praises Miss Bessie indirectly by suggesting that teachers who don't make educational demands on their students are not doing the same excellent job of teaching that she did.

Characterization

Characterization is the description of the people involved in your story. Include details about these people, such as their names, ages, relationship to you, physical appearance and clothing, and actions. Notice how Carl Rowan includes details in describing Miss Bessie.

> "She was only an inch or so above five feet tall and probably never weighed more than 110 pounds in her eighty-five years. . . ."

What do the people in your story think? How do they feel? Add color and depth to your narrative by using direct quotations to show what people say. Including dialogue, the actual words of the people involved, helps the reader know them and makes your story believable.

> "But, Miss Bessie," I complained, "I ain't much interested in *Beowulf*." She fastened on me her large brown eyes that became daggerish slits and said, "Boy, I am your *English* teacher, and I know I've taught you better than this. How dare you talk to me with 'I ain't' this and 'I ain't' that?"

Setting

The **setting** is the time and the place the story happens. Simply telling where and when a story occurs may be enough. Since most readers are familiar with a high school, Rowan does not describe his school but simply states:

> ". . . the woman who taught me English, literature, history, civics, and a lot more than I realized when I attended Bernard High from 1938 to 1942."

Sometimes a story takes place in a location unfamiliar to readers, or the details of the setting are important to the events of the story. For these narratives, a more extensive description of the setting is necessary.

Developing an Essay

Writing Assignment 7: Writing about Education

Rowan writes about a conversation with his school English teacher, Mrs. Bessie Taylor Gwynn, during which he learns an important lesson. During their talk, Miss Bessie chides him for neglecting his studies to play first-string end on the football team. She challenges Rowan toward a larger goal, assuring him that performing well in education is as important as excelling in athletics. She encourages him to be at the top of his class in both areas. Heeding his teacher's advice, Rowan achieves success as both a scholar and an athlete.

You, as well, have had the opportunity to learn many lessons in school. Like many people, however, you may have had some of your most important learning experiences outside the classroom. You may have had a family member, friend, or neighbor teach you how to drive a car, use a camera, budget your money, or surf the Internet. An employer or coworkers may have helped you master the tasks important in a particular job. Perhaps, through trial and error, you taught yourself how to do something that at first seemed difficult. You may have perfected playing a musical instrument or a sport. You may have become skilled at living on your own; staying cool on a humid, 100-degree afternoon; or driving through a snowstorm. Somewhere other than in a classroom, you most likely have also learned lessons about friendship, love, responsibility, patience, honesty, or some other value. Outside of school through the years, you have learned to do many things with the help of others or on your own.

Write a narrative essay telling how you learned a lesson *outside* the classroom. Include dialogue to enhance your story.

The Writing Process

Visualizing

Prewriting Techniques

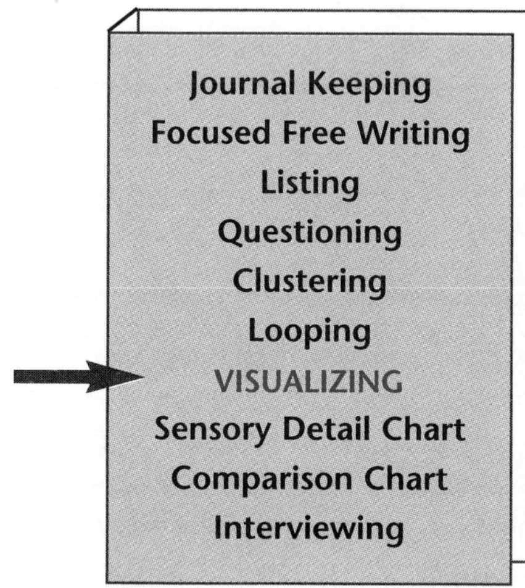

Before television became a household item, millions of people listened to the radio for their entertainment. Since there were no pictures, the radio audience heard words and had to visualize or see in their mind's eye the characters and setting and had to imagine the action.

As a prewriting technique, visualizing is a way to explore a topic. You may visualize while relaxing on a couch, eating by yourself, driving the car, or taking a shower. Let your mind explore events you remember—talk to yourself, coax out the details, take notes, and then write an outline.

An Essay Plan

Read an outline plan.

Title The Education of a Military Man

Thesis I learned from some serious mistakes I made in the military.

I. Topic sentence for first body paragraph	I. I discovered how to survive in the jungle.
A. Major point	A. advice we were given
B. Major point	B. ant attack
C. Major point	C. knowing what leaves to use
II. Topic sentence for second body paragraph	II. I learned about using better judgment.
A. Major point	A. many obstacles—hard terrain
B. Major point	B. finding responsible point man
III. Topic sentence for third body paragraph	III. I learned a life-saving lesson.
A. Major point	A. Miles Gear
B. Major point	B. the attack
C. Major point	C. learning not to get shot

A Model Essay

Read the essay based on the plan.

THE EDUCATION OF A MILITARY MAN

1 Marine Corps Infantry squad leaders are faced in combat with serious decisions that they have to make on their own, without anyone more experienced around to help them. At these times they fall back on previous training and experience acquired at different training camps in the United States and in other countries. One of these military training areas

is Fort Sherman in Panama, the U.S. Army's Jungle Warfare Training Center, situated right next to the north side of the Panama Canal at the Atlantic entrance. Thousands of U.S. Marines and U.S. Army personnel come here every year to do their jungle training. Here as a squad leader, in Second Platoon, Lima Company, Sixth Marine Regiment in the summer of 1998, I had many opportunities to learn from some serious mistakes that I made.

2 During the course of almost two months, we did different types of training, like jungle patrol, land navigation, river crossings, helicopter assaults, and jungle survival. In some of those exercises, I had some experience, so it was not that difficult. Probably the worst of these exercises was the jungle survival course. The Marine Corps put us out into the jungle in teams of two without any supplies besides a small survival kit, which they had us make the day before. Before we left for jungle survival, we were told, "Remember, if you want to complete this exercise successfully, use what you've been taught these last few weeks." Out in the jungle, my first serious mistake was using a certain kind of palm leaf to prepare a bed. What I did not know was the leaves I chose are the fire ant's favorite food. In the night I was awakened by a series of painful ant bites. I learned a valuable lesson that night. The following day, I spent a few hours observing which kinds of leaves the ants did not eat so I could use that kind to make a bed.

3 Training patrols in the jungle is extremely difficult because the rough terrain consists of steep muddy hills and the dense vegetation causes poor visibility. These obstacles greatly reduced our chances of seeing the enemy who might be waiting somewhere along the way. This was why I, as a squad leader, had the responsibility of assigning someone trustworthy to do the job of a point man. Instead, I gave this job to someone who did not pay attention to anything that was happening around him. Somewhere on the way he walked right into a tripwire that set off

a practice booby trap. This explosion is usually a sign for the people who wait in ambush to open fire. Because my point man was not doing his job properly, he had the whole squad "killed." In failing to assign someone trustworthy, I made a mistake that in a real-life situation could have jeopardized the life of every member of my squad. From that time on, I learned to assign a responsible person as point man.

4 The last week in jungle training we did a five-day simulated war, where people use blank ammunition and Miles Gear, a special kind of rifle that consists of a harness, headgear, and a device that goes on the front. This gear enabled us to shoot blank ammunition through our rifles while the device on the front of it shot a laser. If we hit someone else's harness or headgear with this laser, a sensor on the harness would start making a loud whistle noise. Then the controllers knew who had been shot and made those people lie on the ground, pretending to be dead, until the battle was over. On the last day we did an attack on a pretend terrorist camp where the terrorists were holding some civilians hostage. The camp consisted of three buildings with a bunker in the middle of them. My squad was supposed to take out one of the buildings, save the hostages, if there were any, and then attack the bunker. This exercise was a great opportunity to make many mistakes. The first one I made was not having the point man check the door for booby traps, so when he kicked the door in, he was killed. The second mistake was that I shot one of the hostages by accident while I was rushing through the door. The biggest mistake I made was getting myself shot.

5 Before going to Panama I had never had any kind of experience in jungle operations. All my mistakes were valuable because I learned not to make them again. My platoon sergeant said, "We do this kind of training so you can learn from your mistakes because if you ever get into real-life combat, you can't afford to make any." I agree completely.

EXERCISE 3 React to the Narrative Essay

Answer each of the following questions to show your understanding of theses, development, use of quotations, and tone.

1. Why does the writer emphasize setting and events more than characterization? ______________________________

____

____

2. How does the use of direct quotations enhance the essay?

____

3. What details does the writer provide for factual, imaginative, and curious readers?______________________________

____

Work on Writing Assignment 7

EXERCISE 4 Prewrite, Plan, and Draft

Part A

Find a quiet place where you can relax and think about a time when you or someone you know learned a lesson. Try to visualize what happened, the people involved, the place where the event happened, what was said, and what was learned. Take notes.

____

____

____

____

____

____

____

____

Part B

Using the ideas you gathered by visualizing, complete a plan for your essay.

Title ______________________________

Thesis sentence (essay map) ______________________________

____

____

Controlling question ______________________________

Topic Sentence # 1 ______________________________

a. ______________________________

b. ______________________________

c. ______________________________

Topic Sentence # 2 ______________________________

a. ______________________________

b. ______________________________

c. ______________________________

Topic Sentence # 3 ______________________________

a. ______________________________

b. ______________________________

c. ______________________________

Part C

Use your plan to write an essay.

Building Language Skills

Vocabulary

EXERCISE 5 Use the Dictionary

Write the dictionary definitions of the word *profound*.

____

____

____

____

____

____

____

Underline the definition of the word as it is used in the reading selection.

> "I wonder how many teachers today make their students learn the names of officials who spend the public's money and make policies that affect us all so *profoundly*."

EXERCISE 6 Use the Thesaurus

Explain how the meaning of the phrase changes with the use of each synonym.

> "I still made first-string left end and class valedictorian without losing the respect of my ***buddies.***"

1. the respect of my *partners* ______________________________
2. the respect of my *associates* ______________________________
3. the respect of my *allies* ______________________________
4. the respect of my *cronies* ______________________________

Quotations

Consider the difference between the following sentences.

> I complained to Miss Bessie, "I ain't much interested in *Beowulf*."
>
> I complained to Miss Bessie that I wasn't much interested in *Beowulf*.

In the first sentence Rowan's words are quoted exactly. The quotation marks around the words indicate a **direct quotation**.

The second sentence is an **indirect quotation** because the words are not actually spoken. Quotation marks are not used.

Direct: Miss Bessie said, "**I** will not tolerate mediocrity."

Indirect: Miss Bessie said **that she** would not tolerate mediocrity.

Direct: Miss Bessie asked, "Do you have any questions?"

Indirect: Miss Bessie asked if we had any questions.

Several sentences can be quoted with one set of quotation marks.

She said**, "**Boy, you'll make first string only because you have guts and can play football. But do you know what *really* takes guts? Refusing to lower your standards to those of the dumb crowd. It takes guts to say to yourself that you've got to live and be somebody fifty years after these football games are over.**"** (*Note how quotation marks are used at the beginning and at the end of the exact remarks.*)

The position of the speaker in the sentence can vary.

"Get up and tell the class who Frances Perkins is and what you know and think about her," **said Miss Bessie**.

"Get up and tell the class," **Miss Bessie said**, "who Francis Perkins is and what you think about her."

EXERCISE 7 Write Direct Quotations

Change each direct quotation to an indirect quotation.

EXAMPLE

Miss Bessie demanded, "How dare you talk to me that way?"

Miss Bessie demanded that I explain why I was talking to her that way.

1. She said, "I am your English teacher."

____

____

2. She insisted, "You aren't reading enough."

3. My grandmother told me, "You will never forget Miss Bessie."

4. Miss Bessie said, "You get up and tell the class who Frances Perkins is."

5. She said, "You'll make first string only because you have guts."

6. I asked, "How many teachers make their students learn the names of officials?"

Sentence Style

EXERCISE 8 Rearrange Sentences

Rewrite each sentence using the indicated new beginning. Be sure to keep the meaning of the original sentence. Consider the effect of rearranging the words.

1. She would be unforgettable to most of her pupils under any circumstance.

   To most of her pupils ____

2. I remember her with special gratitude and affection.

   Gratefully and ____

3. "Miss Bessie," I said, "I'm trying to make first-string end on the football team."

   I told Miss Bessie ____

4. It was so difficult in those Depression years to focus on much other than getting enough to eat.

   To focus ____

EXERCISE 9 Combine Sentences

Combine the ideas from the sentences in each group to write one new sentence. As you write each sentence, consider the emphasis and relationships you want to achieve.

1.

I had one marvelous teacher.

This teacher forced me to focus on some other things.

____

____

____

2.

I shall never forget one day.

On this day she scolded me.

She said I wasn't reading enough.

I wasn't reading enough of what she wanted me to read.

____

____

____

3.

Americans worry about finding competent teachers.

Americans worry about finding caring teachers.

Americans want these teachers to help their children cope.

____

____

____

4.

An informed teacher is a blessing to children.

A dedicated teacher is a blessing to children.

A informed teacher is an asset to the nation.

A dedicated teacher is an asset to the nation.

____

____

____

Revising the Essay

EXERCISE 10 Rework for Content, Structure, Language, and Accuracy

Part A

Reread your essay to determine if the events, people, and setting are presented in enough detail to make them clear and believable. Revise as necessary.

Part B

1. Circle two different words that can be made more precise. Write in the margin, near each circled word, the new word. Decide whether to use the original word or its synonym.
2. Revise your draft to make sure it includes a direct quotation.
3. Highlight one sentence that can be enhanced by rearranging words. Rewrite the new sentence at the bottom of your paper.

Part C

Using the changes you made in your draft, type a final copy of your paragraph. Proofread your paper to correct misspelled words, typographical errors, and missing words.

CHAPTER 8

Environment

Environment: Exploring the Theme

The weather can play a major role in your well-being. Like many people, you may prefer blue skies and sunny days; sometimes, however, storms come. The selection for Chapter 8 describes a time when the weather turned bad and left an environment that was difficult to live in and a time that was hard to forget.

EXERCISE 1 Prepare to Read

1. What is some of the worst weather you can remember?

____

____

2. In your experience, what happens in a community after a storm?

____

____

____

From *Caught in the Path* by Carolyn Glenn Brewer

ABOUT THE AUTHOR

Social historian Carolyn Glenn Brewer writes an account of the terrible destruction caused by a tornado that destroyed the Kansas City metropolitan area in May 1957. Her perspective is of those, including herself, who lived through the storm. In her book Brewer captures the heartrending drama of the moment of terror as well as of the sustained hope that allowed families to be reunited and communities to be rebuilt.

---

1 In 1957 a tornado destroyed my home. Like a sinister[1] alien it dropped out of a troubled May sky and twisted its way into our lives forever. I was seven years old and didn't know what a tornado was. I had heard the word at school only the week before, but it was an abstract word, with no frame of reference surrounding it. Then on that muggy night in May we survived our thirty seconds of terror. Afterwards my parents sat my five-year-old brother and me down on the kitchen table. My dad went across the street

[1] **sinister** threatening, menacing

to help rescue a woman while my mother looked for shoes in the rubble that had only a few minutes before been our household possessions. Now I heard that awesome word echoing from adult to adult. I looked at my brother and wailed, "This is a tornado?" We both burst into tears.

2 Tornado had many definitions after May 20, 1957: horror, pain, death, plus an incomprehensible[2] tangle of personal business and the frustrating annoyance of reorganizing one's life. But it also came to mean faith, courage and a deep sense of community resurrected[3] out of the rubble, connecting all who shared that anxious night.

3 Those of us who found ourselves in the tornado's path have told our stories over and over again. At block parties and school reunions the subject inevitably comes up. Every spring we stare out office windows at churning skies and remind our coworkers that it can happen here. We tell the stories to our children, so that the tornado's path burrows deeper into our family histories. As with any catastrophic event, legends intertwine with truth, making a fabric of communal experience.

4 Anyone who lived in the Kansas City metropolitan area then has a memory of that night. Even those not directly affected have a story ready when I mention my tornado research. One long-time friend told me his Kansas Boy Scout troop visited stricken Ruskin Heights that summer as a field trip. Another friend said she would never forget the tornado date. Her sister was born that day, and her mother, who was a nurse, wanted to get out of her hospital bed to help the incoming tornado victims. I've heard stories of high school students in Independence giving up their lunch money so they could contribute to the Ruskin High School building fund, and of station-wagon owners enlisted as ambulance drivers.

5 I've often found myself drawn to the John Steuart Curry painting, *Tornado.* A whitish green funnel approaches a Midwestern farmhouse, and I wonder what the children in the painting were doing earlier that day. What favorite toy did they leave behind as they scurried into the storm cellar? I understand the confusion on the little girl's face and the clenched white face of the mother. What was left of their life when it was all over?

6 What I know now is that it is never completely over. My neighborhood was rebuilt within six months, and after a time most of the neighbors moved away, taking their memories with them. Over the years most of the pain faded, leaving a residue of thankfulness. But the total experience of the tornado is still with us. The smell of ozone during a summer storm, the shreds of insulation found between pages of a childhood book remind us that the tornado left a bit of itself with us, making it ours.

[2] **incomprehensible** unfathomable, ungraspable

[3] **resurrected** brought back into notice or use

EXERCISE 2 Reflect on What You Have Read

Finding Facts

1. For how long did the tornado last?

Making Inferences

2. Why did those involved in the tornado repeat their stories over and over again?

Sharing Reactions

3. Should the author's dad have left his family to help rescue a woman across the street?

FOCUSING ON The Descriptive Essay

A descriptive essay depicts or shows the physical details of a place, a person, or a thing. For this kind of essay, your senses must be alert to take in information that you can use to write a clear verbal picture for your reader. Your senses will provide you with an abundance of detail about appearance, sounds, smells, tastes, and textures. The key to writing an effective descriptive essay is to gather the details and then decide what dominant impression you want to create.

Dominant Impression

Your reaction to a powerful storm during the fireworks show on the Fourth of July may have been one of fear; another person's reaction to the same environment may have been one of awe. An overall reaction is called a **dominant impression.** The thesis for a descriptive essay is a sentence that states the dominant impression. For example:

> The storm during the fireworks show was a terrifying ending to the evening.

or

> Nature put on its own beautiful performance with a storm during the fireworks show.

Sensory Details

Sensory details are the kinds of information you gather by paying attention to what you see, hear, smell, taste, and touch. For instance, when you walk down the hall to class, you *see* the shining floor tiles and dull green walls; you *hear* the murmur of teachers talking and the shouts of basketball players announcing a victory; you *feel* the humid warmth of the air inside the building, you *smell* the aroma of cologne and the odor of perspiration, and you may even *taste* the coffee or soda you are carrying with you. To describe a scene vividly, use words that help the reader imagine the environment—picturing the people and settings, seeing the action, hearing the sounds.

Notice the descriptive words Brewer uses:

sight:	a whitish green funnel
touch:	muggy night; out of the rubble
sound:	churning skies
smell:	smell of ozone

"Show" don't "tell"

One of the most effective ways a writer has to convey an image is to "show" not "tell." When you *show,* you use sensory images to describe rather than merely explain.

Telling	As she heard the tornado approach, the scared woman went into the corner of the closet.
Showing	Hearing the roar of the approaching tornado as it swept everything away in its path, the quivering woman huddled in the dark corner of the closet.
Telling	The tornado destroyed all the houses on the street.
Showing	The tornado pummeled the houses into piles of mangled debris.

Developing An Essay

Writing Assignment 8: Writing about Environment

In *Caught in the Path,* Carolyn Glenn Brewer writes about the powerful effects of a tornado. She was only seven when the twister came through her hometown, and the storm lasted for only thirty seconds. This storm and its aftermath, however, made a lasting impression on her and her community. Like Brewer, many people are affected for a lifetime by a destructive storm they experience.

People may also be affected by other aspects of their surroundings. The reaction may be to a single event or to ongoing conditions that occur either outdoors or indoors. For instance, you may react to the outdoors—your neighborhood, the beach, a lakefront scene, a bridge at sunset, a park, your yard on the afternoon of a graduation party. Or you may react to places indoors—your home, a classroom, the shopping mall, a nursing home, visits to your grandparents' house.

Where have you felt comfortable, uncomfortable, scared, nervous, timid, relaxed, exhilarated, calm, serious? What was it about the place and time that influenced your reactions? What specific details can you remember about the experience?

For Writing Assignment 8, describe an environment that affected you.

The Writing Process

Sensory Detail Chart

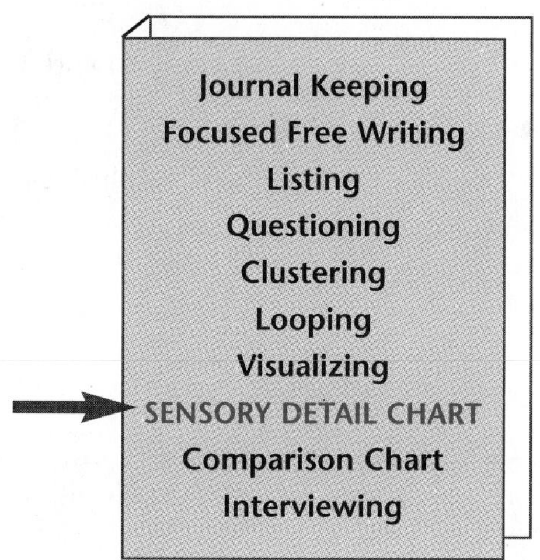

To collect descriptive data about a place, you can use a sensory detail chart. Ask yourself what things you saw, heard, smelled, tasted, or touched to gather specific details.

Look at an example of a completed sensory detail chart that gathers information about childhood visits to grandparents' house.

Sights	Sounds	Smells	Tastes	Textures
green wallpaper	grandma's voice			flocked wallpaper
lamp	storytelling			bronze statue
ornate gates	chimes			iron gates
	nighttime stories	mothballs	chocolate mints	metal rod

Sights	Sounds	Smells	Tastes	Textures
		perfume	white sugar mints	crystal dish
				footprints
old-fashioned clothes				plush carpet
pieces of lace				
board games				

An Essay Plan

Title A Place in My Heart

Thesis My childhood visits to my grandparents' house were enchanting.

I. Topic sentence for first body paragraph	I. Their foyer was elegant.
A. Major point	A. flocked green wallpaper
B. Major point	B. bronze statue of a Roman god
C. Major point	C. wrought iron dining room gates
II. Topic sentence for second body paragraph	II. Their formal living room was enticing.
A. Major point	A. crystal candy dish
B. Major point	B. plush carpeting

III. Topic sentence for third body paragraph
   A. Major point
   B. Major point

III. The bedroom my sister and I shared was wonderful as well.
   A. contents of dresser drawers
   B. nighttime stories

A Model Essay

A PLACE IN MY HEART

1 I close my eyes and see my grandmother's smooth hands moving in the air as she tells me a story. I hear her voice and smell her sweet perfume. I see my grandfather sitting in his favorite chair, reading a book, pencil in hand, listening to music. I am eight years old, and I am in heaven. My childdhood visits to my grandparents' house were enchanting.

2 Without fail, every time I entered the foyer of their home, I was in awe of the elegance. Even the wallpaper was proud. I would secretly run my fingers gently across the green flocked printed flowers on the wallpaper that covered the hallways. Sometimes I would sneak away and sit on the stair landing, staring at the small bronze statue of a Roman god Mercury lifting an ornately beaded lamp. Up the stairway, my dignified ancestors looked on from their gilded frames. Leaning against the flocked wallpaper, I would sit right under the lamp and stare across to the most intricate wrought iron gates that served as dining room doors. I felt like a princess at the entrance of a castle that held the most wonderful surprises.

3 The formal living room was enticing. My sister and I knew the most important thing about that room—at the far end on an end table sat a small crystal dish that held chocolate mints. On some visits, there

would even be extra glass dishes with white sugar mints that would just melt in my mouth. These mints I never got at home. When no one was looking, I would very carefully and quietly, under the pretense of going to the bathroom, tiptoe out into the hall around the stairs to the entranceway of the living room. Since the carpet was always freshly vacuumed before we arrived, I had to be especially clever about sneaking into the room for fear of leaving footprints on the plush carpet. Very carefully, using as little of my foot as possible, I would slip across the room to the candy bowl, grab a sufficient handful and slowly retrace my steps back across the room. If I thought my footprints were too noticeable, I would rub my left hand across the carpet trying to erase the marks so that the carpet still looked freshly vacuumed. I don't know what I thought would happen to me if I had gotten caught, but in retrospect, I'm sure the candy was out there in the living room specifically for us.

4 The bedroom my sister and I shared during visits was wonderful as well. The dresser drawers contained old clothes that smelled of mothballs, ancient yellowed board games, and bits of lace. With patience, my grandmother would pull each and every item out for us telling who in the family had worn what, how to play each game, and what the story was behind a piece of lace. There were fantastic old-fashioned coats and dresses hanging in the closet beneath a shelf that held actual hatboxes. After hearing silly nighttime stories made up by my grandfather, my sister and I all tucked into bed would quietly discuss the adventures we wanted to have the next day. The eight chimes ringing from the grandfather's clock in the foyer would tell me it was morning. I knew it was okay to leave the bedroom to wake my grandparents.

5 My grandparents are no longer with us. Only my memories of a genteel house filled with warmth and love, charming old items and make-believe stories

keep them from fading away. I can still close my eyes, smell the striking mix of perfume and moth balls, and when no one is looking, run my fingers across their velvety green flocked wallpaper.

EXERCISE 3 React to a Descriptive Essay

1. What dominant impression of her grandparents' house does the writer create?

   ____

2. What words in the essay convey this dominant impression?

   ____

   ____

   ____

3. What details in the essay show that the writer is describing the house from a child's perspective?

   ____

   ____

   ____

   ____

   ____

   ____

Work on Writing Assignment 8

EXERCISE 4 Prewrite, Plan, and Draft

Part A

Choose a time when you were particularly aware of your surroundings and complete a sensory detail chart.

Part B

Using the ideas you generated in prewriting, plan your essay.

Thesis (dominant impression) ______________________________

____

____

Controlling question ______________________________

Topic Sentence # 1 ______________________________

a. ______________________________

b. ______________________________

c. ______________________________

Topic Sentence # 2 ______________________________

a. ______________________________

b. ______________________________

c. ______________________________

Topic Sentence # 3 ______________________________

a. ______________________________

b. ______________________________

c. ______________________________

Part C

Use your plan to write your essay.

Building Language Skills

Vocabulary

Word Meanings

EXERCISE 5 Use the Dictionary

Write dictionary definitions of the word *residue*.

____

____

____

____

____

____

____

Underline the definition of the word as it is used in the reading selection.

"Over the years most of the pain faded, leaving a ***residue*** of thankfulness."

Synonyms

EXERCISE 6 Use the Thesaurus

Explain how the meaning of the phrase changes with the use of each synonym.

Over the years most of the pain ***faded,*** leaving a residue of thankfulness.

the pain *faded* ____ the pain *dulled* ______

the pain *vanished* ______

the pain *declined* ______

the pain *withered* ______

Descriptive Words

Descriptive words add meaning to or modify another word in a sentence. Few topics provide as much opportunity for conversation as the weather, yet only two modifiers are commonly used to describe it: "good" or "bad." Some more descriptive words related to weather include:

balmy	frigid	refreshing
crisp	invigorating	searing
enervating	murky	sultry
exhilarating	oppressive	tranquil

EXERCISE 7 Categorize Descriptive Words

Group the modifiers in the preceding columns into two categories. Add two modifiers of your own to each category.

pleasant: *balmy* ______

______

unpleasant: *frigid* ______

______

Descriptive words supply detail.

a sound: explosive, roaring, muffled, discordant, incessant

a city: teeming, thriving, cosmopolitan, bustling, friendly

EXERCISE 8 Supply Descriptive Words

For each word, list five descriptive words.

1. a room: *spacious,* ____________________

2. the wind: *gentle,* ____________________

3. a parking lot: *underground* ____________________

Avoid overused modifiers such as *very, really*, and *so* as well as *good, bad, awful, nice*. When your writing includes fresh, colorful descriptions, your reader is involved in what you have to say. Look at the differences between the sentences in each pair.

1. The tornado dropped out of a **very bad** May sky.

   The tornado dropped out of a **troubled** May sky.

2. Then on that **really sticky** night in May, we survived our thirty seconds of terror.

   Then on that **muggy** night in May, we survived our thirty seconds of terror.

3. The damage was **so horrible.**

   The damage was **catastrophic.**

EXERCISE 9 Choose Descriptive Words

Replace each pair of words with one descriptive word.

EXAMPLE

very large = immense

1. very clean ____________________

2. very cold ____________________

3. very dry ____________________

4. very brilliant ______________________________

5. very tall ______________________________

Notice the effect of the descriptive words in the following sentence:

Violent winds blew through the sleeping town.

The torrid sun shone.

Heavy rain fell from black clouds.

EXERCISE 10 Write Sentences Using Descriptive Words

Rewrite each sentence adding descriptive words.

1. Snow fell on the mountain.

____

2. The tornado moved across the field.

____

3. The breeze blew the trees.

____

Sentence Style

EXERCISE 11 Rearrange Sentences

Rewrite each sentence using the indicated new beginning. Be sure to keep the meaning of the original sentence. Consider the effect of rearranging the words.

1. Like a sinister alien, the tornado dropped out of a troubled May sky and twisted its way into our lives forever.

Dropping out ______________________________

____

____

____

2. Even those not directly affected have a story ready when I mention my tornado research.

   When I mention my tornado research ____________________

   ____

   ____

   ____

3. What favorite toy did they leave behind as they scurried into the storm cellar?

   Scurrying into the storm cellar ________________________

   ____

   ____

   ____

4. What I know now is that it is never completely over.

   Now ____________________________________

   ____

   ____

   ____

EXERCISE 12 Combine Sentences

Combine the ideas from the sentences in each group to write one new sentence. As you write each sentence, consider the emphasis and relationships you want to achieve.

1.

I had heard the word at school.

I had heard the word a week before.

The word was abstract.

____

____

____

____

2.

My dad went across the street.

My dad helped rescue a woman.

____

____

____

3.

Tornado had many definitions after May 20, 1957.

Tornado meant horror.

Tornado meant pain.

Tornado meant death.

____

____

____

____

4.

Over the years, something happened to most of the pain.

Most of the pain faded.

The pain left a residue.

The residue is of thankfulness.

____

____

____

Revising the Essay

EXERCISE 13 Rework for Content, Structure, Language, and Accuracy

Part A

In your draft, underline each sensory detail. Be sure each detail contributes to creating the dominant impression. Add additional details where they are needed.

Part B

1. Circle two different words that can be made more descriptive. Write in the margin, near each circled word, the new word. Decide whether to use the original word or its synonym.
2. Highlight one sentence that can be enhanced by rearranging the words. Rewrite the new sentence at the bottom of your paper.
3. Highlight two sentences that can be made more effective by combining them. Rewrite the new sentence at the bottom of your paper.

Part C

Using the changes you made in your draft, type a final copy of your paragraph. Proofread your paper to correct misspelled words, typographical errors, and missing words.

CHAPTER 9

Perceptions

Perceptions: Exploring the Theme

Silent Dancing: A Partial Remembrance of a Puerto Rican Childhood by Judith Cofer

Focusing on the Comparison Essay

Block Method of Development

Point-by-Point Method of Development

Developing an Essay

Assignment 9: Writing about Perceptions

The Writing Process

Work on Writing Assignment 9

Building Language Skills

Vocabulary

Parallelism

Sentence Style

Revising the Essay

Perceptions: Exploring the Theme

In Chapter 1, you read that memories are like seeds. These memories can be the basis for thinking and writing. Chapter 9 asks the question: How reliable are memories? Because your memories are affected by your perceptions—who you are, what experiences you've had, what insights and beliefs you have—you may remember a situation or event quite differently from someone else. Two people seldom have the same perceptions about the same situation. The author of the selection for Chapter 9 compares the perceptions she has with those of her mother.

EXERCISE 1 Prepare to Read

1. Why do witnesses often tell somewhat different versions of the same happening?

   ____

   ____

2. How do your perceptions about something differ from those of someone you know?

   ____

   ____

   ____

   ____

From *Silent Dancing: A Partial Remembrance of a Puerto Rican Childhood* by Judith Cofer

ABOUT THE AUTHOR

When she was a child, Judith Cofer's father was in the Navy, and her relatives were in both Puerto Rico and New Jersey. As a result, she traveled back and forth frequently from the island to the mainland, having to adjust to two different worlds. In her personal narratives, she describes her bilingual and bicultural experiences. In addition to *Silent Dancing: A Partial Remembrance of a Puerto Rican Childhood*, Judith Cofer has written *Reaching for the Mainland* and *The Line of the Sun*.

MY MEMORY OF FATHER'S HOMECOMING

1 My first memory is of Father's homecoming party and the gift he brought me from San Juan—a pink iron crib like an ornate birdcage—and the sense of abandonment I felt for the first time in my short life as all eyes turned to the handsome stranger in uniform and away from me in my frilly new dress and patent leather shoes, trapped inside my pink iron crib, screaming my head off for *Mami, Tia, Mama Nanda,* anybody . . . to come lift me out of my prison.

2 When I ask about the events of that day, my mother still rolls her eyes back and throws her hands up in a gesture of dismay. The story varies with the telling and the teller, but it seems that I climbed out of my tall crib on my own and headed for the party in the backyard. The pig was on the spit and the beer was flowing. In the living room the Victrola was playing my father's Elvis Presley records loudly. (*I may have imagined this.*) My mother is sitting on his lap. She is gorgeous in the red silk dress he has given her. There is a circle of people around him. Everyone is having a good time. And everyone has forgotten about me. I see myself slipping through the crowd and into flames. Immediately, I am pulled out by a man's strong hands. No real damage: my abundant hair is a little singed,[1] but that is all. Mother is crying. I am the center of everyone's attention once again. Even *his.*

The Last Word

3 "You were the happiest little girl on the island, I believe," she says smiling down at his picture. "After a few days of getting acquainted, you two were inseparable. He took you everywhere with him."

4 "Mother..." In spite of my resolve, I am jarred by the disparity[2] of our recollections of this event. "Was there a party for him when he returned? Did you roast a pig out in the backyard? I remember a fire . . . and an accident involving me."

5 She lifts her eyes to meet mine. She looks mildly surprised.

6 "You were only a baby . . . what is it that you think happened on that day?"

7 "I remember that I was put in a crib and left alone. I remember many people talking, music, laughter." I want her to finish the story. I want my mother to tell me that what I remember is true. But she is stubborn, too. Her memories are precious to her, and although she accepts my explana-

[1] **singed** burned, scorched

[2] **disparity** difference

tions that what I write in my poems and stories is mainly the product of my imagination, she wants certain things she believes are true to remain sacred, untouched by my fictions.

8 "And what is this accident you remember? What do you think happened at your father's homecoming party?" Her voice has taken on the deadly serious tone that has always made me swallow hard. I am about to be set straight. I decide to forge ahead. *This is* just *an experiment*, I tell myself. I am comparing notes on the past with my mother. This can be managed without resentment. After all, we are both intelligent adults.

9 "I climbed out of the crib, and walked outside. I think . . . I fell into the fire." My mother shakes her head. She is now angry, and worse, disappointed in me. She turns the pages of the book until she finds my birthday picture. A short while after his return from Panama, my father is supposed to have spent a small fortune giving me the fanciest birthday party ever seen in our pueblo. He wanted to make up for all the good times together we had missed. My mother has told me the story dozens of times. There are many photographs documenting the event. Every time I visit a relative, someone brings out an album and shows me a face I've memorized: that of a very solemn two-year-old dressed in a fancy dress sent by an aunt from New York just for the occasion, surrounded by toys and decorations, a huge, ornate cake in front of me. I am not smiling in any of these pictures.

10 My mother turns the album toward me. "Where were you burned?" she asks, letting a little irony[3] sharpen the hurt in her voice. "Does that look like a child who was neglected for one moment?"

11 "So what really happened on that day, Mami?" I look at the two-year-old's face again. There is a celebration going on around her, but her eyes—and my memory—tell me that she is not a part of it.

12 "There was a little accident involving the fire that day, Hija," my mother says in a gentler voice. She is the Keeper of the Past. As the main witness of my childhood, she has the power to refute[4] my claims.

13 "This is what happened. You were fascinated by a large book your father brought home from his travels. I believe it was a foreign language dictionary. We couldn't pry[5] it away from you, though it was almost as big as you. I took my eyes off you for one moment, *un momentito, nada mas, Hija,* and you somehow dragged that book to the pit where we were roasting a pig, and you threw it in."

14 "Do you know why I did that, Mother?" I am curious to hear her

[3] **irony** mockery, sarcasm, humor

[4] **refute** oppose, contradict, debate

[5] **pry** move, push, hoist

explanation. I dimly recall early mentions of a valuable book I supposedly did away with in the distant past.

15 "Why do children do anything they do? The fire attracted you. Maybe you wanted attention. I don't know. But," she shakes her finger at me in mock accusation, "if you remember a burning feeling, the location of this fire was your little behind after I gave you some *pan-pan* to make sure you didn't try anything like that ever again."

16 We both laugh at her use of the baby word for a spanking that I had not heard her say in three decades.

17 "That is what really happened?"

18 "*Es le papa verdad,*" she says. "Nothing but the truth."

19 But that is not how I remember it.

EXERCISE 2 Reflect on What You Have Read

Finding Facts

1. How old is the author when her father returns from Panama?

___

Making Inferences

2. Why does the author describe her new crib as an "ornate birdcage"?

___

___

___

___

Sharing Reactions

3. Cofer calls her mother the "Keeper of the Past." What does Cofer mean? Do you agree? Explain.

___

___

___

___

FOCUSING ON The Comparison Essay

One person's perceptions of what happened at a given time came be quite different from another person's perceptions. Judith Cofer remembers the evening of her father's return from Panama quite differently from the way her mother remembers it. Comparing these perceptions can help the reader learn something about the daughter and her mother. Cofer, as a two-year-old, seems to have felt left out as attention turned from her to her father. Her mother, on the other hand, does not want to believe that she neglected her child.

How are things compared?

Comparing or analyzing how things are alike and different, is an important way of presenting information. Learning is often a result of comparing something new with something familiar. In teaching a child about a skunk, you might say, "Yes, dear, a skunk is like a kitten except. . . ." By comparing the qualities of various makes of automobiles, colleges, or computers, you can learn the differences in quality, practicality, affordability, and the like.

Using comparison in essay writing is an effective way of presenting an opinion about how things are similar to or different from each other. To get started comparing, you will want to make a chart showing the qualities or characteristics of each item or issue to be discussed.

The following chart compares working at a gas station with attending college.

Points	Subject A: Service Station	Subject B: College
tasks	pumping gas changing oil fixing flats	completing assignments writing papers studying for tests
environment	garage co-workers	classroom facility
time	regular shifts	open-ended

Using the items on the chart, the writer has several options for organizing an essay.

BLOCK METHOD OF DEVELOPMENT

The block method of development, sometimes called AB method, means writing first about one subject of the comparison (A) and then writing about the second subject of the comparison (B).

Thesis Working at the service station is more predictable than taking courses at the local college.

Subject A
Point 1
Point 2
Point 3

Subject A—Body Paragraph 1

Topic Sentence Working at the service station is predictable.

1. routine tasks
2. familiar environment
3. definite work hours

Subject B
Point 1
Point 2
Point 3

Subject B—Body Paragraph 2

Topic Sentence Taking courses at college is unpredictable.

1. variable academic demands
2. new courses each semester
3. open-ended study time

POINT-BY-POINT METHOD OF DEVELOPMENT

The point-by-point method of development deals with both topics of comparison in each body paragraph. The topic sentence of the paragraph shows the point of comparison.

Thesis Working at the service station is more predictable than taking courses at the local college.

Point 1
Subject A
Subject B

Point 1—Body Paragraph

Topic Sentence Working at a service station is more routine than attending college.

A. station – pumping gas, changing oil
B. college – assignments, tests

Point 2
Subject A
Subject B

Point 2—Body Paragraph

Topic Sentence The environment at the service station is more familiar than at college.

A. station – garage, co-workers

B. college – classroom, faculty

Point 3
Subject A
Subject B

Point 3—Body Paragraph

Topic Sentence My time commitment is more definite at work than at college.

A. station – regular shifts

B. college – varies

Which method of organization should you use for a comparison essay?

As you might expect, you use the method that best suits your topic. If your topic is relatively simple and easy to follow, you can use the block method. Readers are able to remember the points you made in the first section as they read the second; as they finish the essay, they can follow your conclusion.

If the topic is more complex and involved or you want to detail carefully the information you present, you use the point-by-point method. This method allows you to be specific about one point and show how it affects the subjects or issues being compared. Then you go on to the second point to show how it applies to each subject. The reader considers how a point relates to each subject before going on to a new point.

What transition words are used for writing a comparison essay?

The following words are helpful in clarifying similarities and differences:

Comparison	Contrast
also	however
similarly	in contrast
too	on the contrary
both	although
like	but
in the same manner	instead of
not only . . . but also	unlike
share the same	on the other hand

Developing an Essay

Assignment 9: Writing about Perceptions

Judith Cofer writes about differences between her and her mother's perceptions of an event that happened long ago. Comparing these differences illuminates the nature of their family interrelationships.

You may compare your perceptions about two different persons, places, or ideas. Which of your parents is the more effective disciplinarian? Which of the two coaches was more helpful to you? Which friend handles problems more effectively? Do you prefer living in the city or in the suburbs? Is living in a dorm better than living at home or living in an apartment? Do you prefer individual or team sports? Is living alone preferable to living with a partner? Is communicating by e-mail preferable to using the phone? Do you prefer eating at home to eating in a restaurant? Do you prefer having a dog or a cat as a pet? Is watching a move in the theater more satisfying than watching a video at home? Your answer to any one of these questions will provide the basis for a comparative essay.

The assignment for Chapter 9 is to write an essay comparing two different people, places, or ideas.

The Writing Process

Comparison Chart

Prewriting Techniques

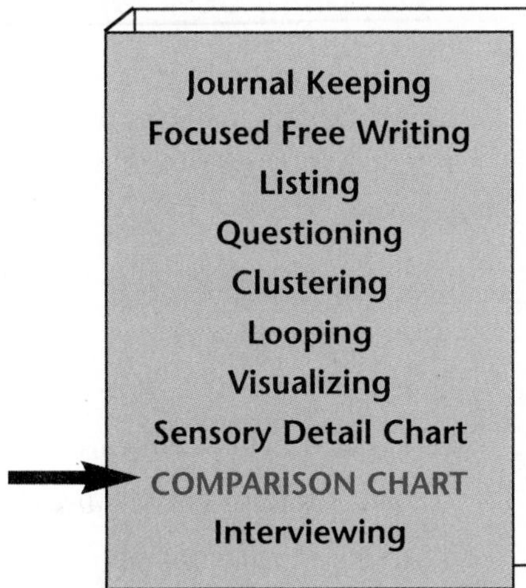

To create a comparison chart, first make a box with a number of columns and rows. At the top of the column heading write the subject you will be comparing.

The most critical part of setting up the chart is determining what points of comparison to write in the first column. These points form the basis for a thesis and support.

Look at how a writer uses a comparison chart to compare two jobs he had in high school.

Points	Subject A Stacking Hay at Farm	Subject B Moving Boxes and Furniture for Moving Company
environment	backbreaking very hot horrible smells monotonous	strenuous challenging variety
interaction	hardly any talk old hay hands	constant interchange crew, driver, customers
wages	$6 per hour	$6 per hour plus bonuses

An Essay Plan

Title Furniture Moves Easier Than Hay

Thesis Without a doubt, I preferred the work at the moving company to the job at the farm.

METHOD OF DEVELOPMENT	POINT-BY-POINT METHOD
Point 1 Topic Sentence	I. Although both jobs were physically tough, moving hay was far more demanding than moving furniture.
Subject A	A. Farm
1. Supporting detail	1. throwing hay backbreaking work
2. Supporting detail	2. intense heat
3. Supporting detail	3. manure smell
Subject B	B. Local moving company
1. Supporting detail	1. hard exercise moving heavy objects
2. Supporting detail	2. tricky maneuvers with items
3. Supporting detail	3. different challenges

Point 2 Topic Sentence	II. The loneliness of hauling hay made the job less enjoyable than moving furniture and boxes.
Subject A	A. Farm
1. Supporting detail	1. hay hands a lot older
2. Supporting detail	2. not much talking
Subject B	B. Local moving company
1. Supporting detail	1. moving crew my age and older
2. Supporting detail	2. driver
3. Supporting detail	3. customers
Point 3 Topic Sentence	III. Monetarily, I earned the same pitching hay as hauling boxes, but the perks involved in moving were greater.
Subject A	A. Farm
1. Supporting detail	1. $6 per hour
2. Supporting detail	2. no extras
B. Subject #2	B. Local moving company
1. Supporting detail	1. $6 per hour
2. Supporting detail	2. customers' tips
3. Supporting detail	3. customers gave away things

A Model Essay

Point-By-Point

FURNITURE MOVES EASIER THAN HAY

1 When I was very young I shoveled neighbors' walkways for a few dollars. Later on, I got a newspaper route pitching papers to the neighbors' front doors. One summer I was a "gofer" for a roofing company, and another, I caddied at a local golf course. Two jobs that I remember most vividly,

though, were stacking hay at a friend's farm the summer before my senior year and working part time for a local moving company. Without a doubt, I preferred the work at the moving company to the job at the farm.

2 Although both jobs were physically tough, moving hay was far more demanding than moving furniture. Throwing heavy hay into the barn loft was backbreaking work. After pitching bales, weighing between 60 and 100 pounds each, into the air ten feet or more to build stacks to the roof, I felt every part of my arms, shoulders, and back throb. In the intense heat, lifting each load became almost unbearable. During the hottest part of the year, the temperature inside the barn was at least 20 degrees hotter than outside, and the air reeked from manure. Every day, I came home in sweat-drenched, smelly clothes. Moving furniture, too, gave me plenty of hard exercise. The other guys taught me how to stack two, three boxes on my back to carry up the stairs. Moving large, awkward pieces was a physical strain. I didn't need to deal with intense heat and odor, however, and every day brought different challenges. I definitely preferred the environment and variety involved in moving furniture to the discomfort and monotony of throwing hay.

3 The loneliness of hauling hay made the job less enjoyable than moving furniture and boxes. At the farm, I worked beside men who were two or three times my age. The hay hands, as they're called, didn't talk except to grunt directions when necessary. Occasionally, the silence would be broken with one of them saying, "Git the salt," and we'd sprinkle a layer of salt to help prevent spontaneous combustion. Companionship was not a part of the job. In contrast, while working for the moving company, I got to interact with the crew members and the driver. The crew members, mostly in their twenties and older, liked to tell jokes and tease each another about one thing or another. The driver was responsible for the condition of the furniture, so he'd tell us exactly

how he wanted us to pad things and maneuver them through tight doorways, up or down the stairs, or around a corner. Overall, compared with the isolation of haying, I really enjoyed the companionship that came with moving furniture.

4 Although monetarily, at $6 an hour I earned about the same pitching hay as hauling boxes, the perks involved in moving were greater. As much as I disliked working at the farm, it never occurred to me to quit. I stuck with the job, and by the end of the summer, I had enough money to buy a used car. Even though I also earned $6 per hour as a mover's helper, the job was overall more rewarding. Most people were so appreciative after we did a good job moving their belongings that they would give the driver a generous tip to split among us. Other times, customers gave away things that they did not need or want anymore. I certainly wouldn't become a rich man doing either job, but carrying furniture brought more bonuses than stacking hay bales.

5 I don't lift for wages now, but if I were to go back to that kind of work, I am sure that I would chose moving furniture over stacking hay. I am glad the uncomfortable environment, the limited interaction with others, and the minimal salary of the hay field are in the past. I wouldn't mind, however, getting into shape again as a mover.

EXERCISE 3 React to a Comparison Essay

1. **Underline the transition words that are used in the essay to show comparison and contrast.**

2. **Using the outline on page 202 as a guide, write an outline showing how the essay could be developed using the block method.**

Subject A

I. Topic Sentence

Point 1

Point 2

Point 3

Subject B

II. Topic Sentence

Point 1

Point 2

Point 3

Work on Writing Assignment 9

EXERCISE 4 Prewrite, Plan, and Draft

Part A

Make a comparison chart for your topic.

Points	Subject A	Subject B

Part B

1. Based on the information you have gathered in your chart, write a thesis sentence comparing your two subjects.

____

____

2. What is the controlling question your essay will answer?

____

____

3. Based on your thesis sentence, develop two plans—block method and point-by-point method—for organizing your ideas.

Block Method

Block A—BODY PARAGRAPH 1

A
Point 1
Point 2
Point 3

Topic Sentence ____

____

____

____

____

____

Block B—BODY PARAGRAPH 2

B
Point 1
Point 2
Point 3

Topic Sentence ____

____

____

____

____

____

Point-By-Point Method

Point 1—BODY PARAGRAPH

Point 1
A
B

Topic Sentence ____

____

____

____

____

Point 2—BODY PARAGRAPH

Point 2
A
B

Topic Sentence ______________________________

____

____

____

____

Point 3—BODY PARAGRAPH

Point 3
A
B

Topic Sentence ______________________________

____

____

____

____

____

Part C

Use the plan you prefer to write a draft of an essay. Give your essay a title.

Building Language Skills

Vocabulary

Word Meanings

EXERCISE 5 Use the Dictionary

Write dictionary definitions of the word *forge*.

____

____

Underline the definition of the word as it is used in the following sentence:

"I decide to **forge** ahead."

Synonyms

EXERCISE 6 Use the Thesaurus

Explain how the meaning of the phrase changes with the use of each synonym.

"The face of a very **solemn** two-year-old dressed in a fancy dress . . ."

1. **solemn** two-year-old ______
2. **sad** two-year-old ______
3. **glum** two-year-old ______
4. **humorless** two-year-old ______

Parallelism

If your job responsibilities are similar to those of someone else, you have parallel responsibilities. Lists of your responsibilities would be alike. The word "parallel" can also be applied to sentence structure. Parts of a sentence that are in a series need to be written in the same form or structure so that a reader can easily detect that they serve the same function.

In the following sentences notice that the italicized sections are lists or series and therefore have the same form or structure.

1. In writing about one's life, one often has to rely on that combination of *memory*, *imagination*, and *strong emotion* that may result in "poetic truth."

    memory

    imagination

    (strong) emotion

2. In preparing to write her memoirs Virginia Woolf said, "*I dream*; *I make up pictures of a summer's afternoon*."

This is a list of two items. Each item is an independent clause.

    I dream.

    I make up pictures of a summer's afternoon.

3. There are *birth*, *marriage*, and *death* certificates on file.

In this sentence, there are three words modifying "certificates."

    birth

    marriage

    death

4. There are *letters* and *family photographs* in someone's *desk* or *attic*.

In this sentence, there are two sets of words that are parallel.

    letters

    family photographs

and

    desk

    attic

Why is parallelism important?

If similar parts of a sentence are not in the same form, the sentence is difficult to read, and the meaning may be unclear.

> In writing about one's life, one often has to rely on that combination of *memory*, *using imagination*, and *strong emotion* that may result in "poetic truth."

When the parts in a series are lined up, the word "using" sticks out, indicating that the sentence parts are not parallel.

memory

using imagination

strong emotion

One way to revise the sentence is to remove "using."

One's life, one often has to rely on that combination of *memory*, *imagination*, and *strong emotion* that may result in "poetic truth."

Another way to revise the sentence is to use the following parallel parts:

depending on memory

using imagination

experiencing strong emotion

In writing about one's life, one often has to rely on that combination of *depending on memory*, *using imagination*, and *experiencing strong emotion* that may result in "poetic truth."

Look at another example.

Relatives assign themselves the role of *genealogist* or being *family bard.*

When the parts in a series are lined up, the word "being" sticks out, indicating it needs to be eliminated.

genealogist

being family bard

Using parallel structure, you might rewrite

Relatives assign themselves the role of *genealogist* or *family bard.*

EXERCISE 7 Create Parallel Structure

Part A

Underline in each sentence the parts that are parallel and list them. Add to the list another parallel part that could be included in the sentence.

EXAMPLE

The events can be projected on a light blue screen, the hurtful parts can be edited out, and the moments of joy can be brought in sharp focus to the foreground.

the events can be projected on a light blue screen ____________________

the hurtful parts can be edited out ____________________

the moments of joy can be brought in sharp focus to the foreground _____

the times of laughter can be enjoyed by us ____________________

1. It is difficult to single out my mother as she really was, to imagine what she was thinking, or to put a single sentence into her mouth.

____

____

____

____

2. Many bright colors, many distinct sounds, are several violent moments of being are part of a rough visual description of childhood.

____

____

____

____

3. This is how I shape it and how l see myself as a child.

____

Part B

Edit each of the following sentences to eliminate any errors in parallelism; then write the parallel parts in the spaces following the sentence to show their parallelism.

1. What compels some of us to examine and reexamining our lives in poems?

2. I wanted the essays to be not just family history, but also to be making creative explorations of known territory.

3. My first memory is of Father's homecoming party, of the gift from San Juan and feeling the sense of abandonment.

Sentence Style

EXERCISE 8 Rearrange Sentences

Rewrite each sentence using the indicated new beginning. Be sure to keep the meaning of the original sentence. Consider the effect of rearranging the words.

1. I am not, in my poetry and my fiction writing, a slave to memory.

   In my poetry ______________________________

   ____

   ____

2. He left for Panama when I was a couple of months pregnant with you and didn't get back until you were two years old.

   I was ______________________________

   ____

   ____

3. I have my own "memories" about this time in my life, but I decide to ask her a few questions anyway.

   I decide to ______________________________

   ____

   ____

4. There are few pictures of him in middle age in her album.

   Her album contains ______________________________

   ____

   ____

EXERCISE 9 Combine Sentences

Combine the ideas from the sentences in each group to write one new sentence. As you write each sentence, consider the emphasis and relationships you want to achieve.

1.

My mother opens the photo album.

There is a picture.

The picture shows my father.

The picture shows a very young man.

The young man is wearing an army uniform.

____

____

____

____

2.

Her voice has taken on the serious tone.

Her voice has taken on the deadly tone.

The tone has always made me swallow hard.

____

____

____

____

3.

Does that look like a child?

The child was neglected.

The child was neglected for one moment.

____

____

____

____

4.

I ask about the events of that day.

My mother still rolls her eyes back.

My mother throws her hands up in a gesture of dismay.

____

____

____

____

Revising the Essay

EXERCISE 10 Rework for Content, Structure, Language, and Accuracy

Part A

Reread your essay underlining transition words that show comparison. Add additional transitions as needed.

Part B

1. Circle two different words that can be made more specific. Next to each circled word, write in the margin your revised word. Decide whether to use the original word or its synonym.

2. Underline a parallel construction that you have used in your essay. If you don't have one, add one. Rewrite any sentences that need correction for lack of parallelism.
3. Highlight one sentence that can be enhanced by rearranging words. Rewrite the new sentence at the bottom of your paper.
4. Highlight two sentences that can be made more effective by combining them. Rewrite the new sentence at the bottom of your paper.

Part C

Proofread your paper to correct misspelled words, typographical errors, and missing words. Using the revisions you made on your draft, type a final copy of your essay.

CHAPTER 10

Time

Time: Exploring the Theme

What do you do with the seven days or 168 hours you have each week? The author of the selection for Chapter 10 attempts to persuade readers that for health and sanity, time should be spent with family and friends, apart from the workaday world. He provides reasons for believing as he does.

EXERCISE 1 Prepare to Read

1. How do you make decisions about what to do with your time?

____

____

2. What is "time well spent"?

____

____

____

From *Sabbath: Remembering the Sacred Rhythm of Rest and Delight* by Wayne Muller

ABOUT THE AUTHOR

An ordained minister, a therapist, and an author, Wayne Muller has, for the last twenty-five years, worked with some of the most disadvantaged members of society. He is the founder of Bread for the Journey, a national nonprofit charity serving the poor and underprivileged. He has written *Legacy of the Heart: The Spiritual Advantages of a Painful Childhood* and *Then, How Shall We Live?* in addition to *Sabbath: Remembering the Sacred Rhythm of Rest and Delight.*

---

1 In the relentless business of modern life, we have lost the rhythm between action and rest. As the founder of a public charity, I visit the offices of wealthy donors, crowded social service agencies, and the small homes of the poorest families. Remarkably, within this mosaic there is a universal refrain: "I am so busy." I speak with people in business and education, doctors and day-care workers, shopkeepers and social workers, parents and teachers, nurses and lawyers, students and therapists, community activists and cooks—the weary, overwhelmed, and lost. Despite our good hearts and

equally good intentions, our life and work rarely feel light, pleasant, or healing. Instead, as it all piles endlessly upon itself, the whole experience of being alive begins to melt into one enormous obligation. It becomes the standard greeting everywhere: "I am so busy."

2 We say this to one another with no small degree of pride, as if our exhaustion were a trophy, our ability to withstand stress a mark of real character. The busier we are, the more important we seem to ourselves and, we imagine, to others. To be unavailable to our friends and family, to be unable to find time for the sunset (or even to know that the sun has set at all), to whiz through our obligations without time for a single mindful breath—this has become the model of a successful life.

3 Because we do not rest, we lose our way. We miss the compass points that show us where to go. We lose the nourishment that gives us succor.[1] We miss the quiet that gives us wisdom. Poisoned by the hypnotic belief that good things come only through tireless effort, we never truly rest. And for want of rest, our lives are in danger.

4 How have we allowed this to happen? This was not our intention; this is not the world we dreamed of when we were young and life seemed full of possibility and promise. How did we get so terribly rushed in a world saturated with work and responsibility, yet somehow bereft[2] of joy and delight?

5 I suggest it is this: We have forgotten the Sabbath.

6 Most spiritual traditions prescribe some kind of Sabbath, time consecrated to enjoy and celebrate what is beautiful and good—time to light candles, sing songs, worship, tell stories, bless our children and loved ones, give thanks, share meals, nap, walk, and even make love. It is time to be nourished and refreshed as we let our work, our chores, and our important projects lie fallow,[3] trusting that there are larger forces at work taking care of the world when we are at rest.

7 Sabbath time is a revolutionary challenge to the violence of overwork because it honors the necessity of dormancy.[4] If certain plant species do not lie dormant during winter, the plant begins to die off. Rest is not just a psychological convenience; it is a spiritual and biological necessity. Perhaps this is why, in most spiritual traditions, "Remember the Sabbath" is more than simply a lifestyle suggestion. It is a commandment, an ethical precept as serious as prohibitions against killing, stealing, and lying.

8 Sabbath is more than the absence of work; it is a day when we partake of

[1] **succor** comfort, support
[2] **bereft** deprived of, lacking
[3] **fallow** incomplete, unfulfilled
[4] **dormancy** rest, sleep, inactivity

the wisdom, peace, and delight that grow only in the soil of time—time consecrated specifically for play, refreshment, and renewal. Many of us, in our desperate drive to be successful and care for our many responsibilities, feel terrible guilt when we take time to rest. But the Sabbath has proven its wisdom over the ages. The Sabbath gives us the permission we need to stop, to restore our souls. As part of the Judeo-Christian tradition, it is already woven into the fabric of our society. Many of us still recall when, not long ago, shops and offices were closed on Sundays. Those quiet Sunday afternoons are embedded in our cultural memory.

9 Much of modern life is specifically designed to seduce our attention away from Sabbath rest. When we are in the world with our eyes wide open, the seductions are insatiable.[5] Hundreds of channels of cable and satellite television; phones with multiple lines and call waiting, begging us to talk to more than one person at a time; mail, e-mail, and overnight mail; fax machines; billboards; magazines; newspapers; radio. For those of us with children, there are endless soccer practices, baseball games, homework, laundry, housecleaning, and errands. Every responsibility, every stimulus competes for our attention: Buy me. Do me. Watch me. Try me. Drink me. It is as if we have inadvertently[6] stumbled into some horrific wonderland.

10 The point is not to return to some forced, legalistic Sabbath. We rightfully chafe against the dreary and humorless Sundays that obscured[7] the more traditional healing prescriptions of companionship and laughter. A new Sabbath must invite a conversation about the forgotten necessity of rest. Sabbath may be a holy day, an afternoon, an hour, a walk—*anything* that preserves the experience of life-giving repose and nourishment. During Sabbath, we take our hand from the plow and let the earth care for things, while we drink, if just briefly, from the fountain of rest and delight.

11 I make a plea for renewed Sabbath-keeping. As a nation, we cannot live like this, endlessly rushing about in a desperate frenzy, never stopping to enjoy the blessings of family and friends, unable to taste the fruits of life. We can change society by beginning a quiet revolution of change in ourselves and our families. Let us take a collective breath, rest, pray, meditate, walk, sing, eat, and take time to share the unhurried company of those we love. Let us, for just one day, cease[8] our desperate striving for more, and instead taste the blessings we have already been given, and give thanks. Religious traditions agree on this: God does not want us to be exhausted; God wants us to be happy. And so let us remember the Sabbath.

[5] **insatiable** unappeasable, gluttonous, unable to be satisfied or fulfilled

[6] **inadvertently** unintentionally, accidentally

[7] **obscured** hid, covered, masked

[8] **cease** stop

EXERCISE 2 Reflect on What You Have Read

Finding Facts

1. What is the standard greeting of today? ______________________________

____

Making Inferences

2. How is Sabbath time more than the absence of work?

____

____

____

Sharing Reactions

3. Why is it that many people today live in a "horrific wonderland"?

____

____

____

____

____

FOCUSING ON The Persuasive Essay

When you persuade, you do more than express an opinion. You attempt to convince others to change their minds. You ask them to accept the view you present to them and perhaps even to do something differently because of this new view. Persuasion is a part of daily life. You may ask an instructor for extra time to complete a paper. You try to convince friends to spend time studying with you or to see a particular movie with you. You persuade a sales associate to let you make a purchase even though the store has just closed for the day. In writing, likewise, you share a view that you want your readers to accept.

Argumentation and Persuasion

One kind of persuasion, called **argumentation,** is based on statistics and other factual information. Argumentation depends solely on reason and logic. Many papers for academic courses require this approach to persuasion. For these papers, you need to do research to locate details that support your position and to use endnotes to show the sources of information you use.

In a broader sense, **persuasion** appeals to both reason and emotion. In fact, Wayne Muller appeals largely to the feelings of readers in his writing. Because he believes they are stressed about not having enough time, he suggests ways to spend time more wisely. His writing is not based on research but on details from his observation and general knowledge. The purpose of persuasive writing is to let your readers know what you know and to appeal to them to believe as you do or act as you would like them to act.

In persuasive writing, you have a special need to consider your audience. By taking some time to think about your readers, what they already know and believe and what view they are likely to have on your topic, you have an idea about how to go about trying to change their opinion. You know what information they will need and what emotional appeals are likely to be effective.

Point of View

You have choices about how you will present your ideas. You may want to use the "I" perspective or first person as Muller does. "**I** make a plea for renewed Sabbath-keeping. As a nation, **we** cannot live like this. . . ." Using the first person puts the focus on you, the writer. What you write is clearly from your personal point of view. You may want to use the "you" perspective or second person. Using "you" in the first sentence of this paragraph and throughout the text, indicates that the writer is talking directly to the reader. This perspective is often used to give instructions. "You" is also commonly used in conversation and informal writing. Another point of view uses neither "I" nor "you," but gives information objectively using "he," "she," "it," "they," and related pronouns. This type of perspective—one that does not name the writer or the reader but focuses on others—is used in argumentation and other academic papers. In this textbook, you have focused on using the personal "I" and telling about yourself. "You" is rarely used in academic writing. "He/she/they" is common in academic and professional writing.

Once you decide on your point of view, be sure not to confuse your readers by changing to another perspective.

POINT OF VIEW

Point of View	Pronouns Used	Focus	Example
First Person	I, me, we, us	The writing is focused on the writer.	*I spend my time wisely.*
Second Person	you	The writing is focused on the reader.	*You spend your time wisely.*
Third Person	she, her, he, him, it, they, them	The writing is focused on neither the writer or the reader.	*They spend their time wisely.*

Persuasive Details

To develop the body paragraphs, you present both logical and emotional appeals. The support for your body paragraphs can include any of the kinds of writing you have used in this text: examples, description, narration, comparison/contrast, and persuasion. In persuasion, as in most essays, a combination of techniques can be effective.

Sensory detail and precise language help readers to understand your position and agree with you. Be clear and direct. Why should readers accept what you say, believe as you do? How can readers take the action you want them to take?

The order of your supporting points is important. Most likely, you will develop the body of your essay using persuasive order of importance. If you have three body paragraphs, each developing a point, decide which is your most compelling point, which is the second most, and which the least. You may want to start with your second most important point in the first body paragraph so the reader is impressed at the start. Then put your weakest point in the next or middle body paragraph. This position is the least prominent. Finally, in the last paragraph of your body, emphasize your most important reason. The point you make in the last body paragraph is the one that your readers will remember.

When you have completed your persuasive essay, read it as your readers will read it. Have you clearly and honestly shared your position? Will readers who begin reading from a perspective different from yours come to believe as you do?

PERSUASIVE ORDER

Body Paragraph 1	Second Most Important Support Point
Body Paragraph 2	Least Important Point
Body Paragraph 3	Most Important Point

Developing an Essay

Assignment 10: Writing about an Issue

Wayne Muller writes to persuade readers to believe as he does. He thinks that time is well used for rest, prayer, meditation, walking, singing, eating, and sharing the unhurried company of those we love. Trying to convince readers to share his opinion, he gets them involved in the issue, giving reasons to believe as he does.

You, too, are likely to have opinions on a variety of topics. For you, for example, what is time well spent or not well spent? How important is taking time for yourself or taking time to volunteer for a worthwhile cause? Is the good life being single, married, or living with someone? Should people remain childless or have only one child? What is important in effective parenting? Do you advise being a foster parent? Adopting a child? How important is graduating from high school or attending college? What learning is vital in a good education? What advice do you have about using drugs, smoking cigarettes, exercising, driving a car? Should others consider working where you do? Shopping where you do? Taking up a particular career? Do you recommend a particular hobby? What places have you been that other people would enjoy seeing? What advice can you give? Which of your opinions is of value for others?

For Writing Assignment 10, write about an issue important to you. Choose a point of view—"I," "you," or "he, she, they"—and keep this perspective consistent throughout your essay.

The Writing Process

Interviewing

Prewriting Techniques

Journal Keeping
Focused Free Writing
Listing
Questioning
Clustering
Looping
Visualizing
Sensory Detail Chart
Comparison Chart
→ INTERVIEWING

How do reporters get their stories? They rely on interviews with key people. Similarly, when you are gathering ideas for an essay, you may find it useful to talk with those who have information you need. Before your conversation, make a list of questions. Take notes during the interview or get permission to record the session, and you can gather valuable data for your essay.

An application of this technique is to have someone interview you so that you can think aloud about a topic. Informally, you use this process when you discuss a writing assignment with others.

Study the kinds of questions that are useful in interviewing and the kinds of notes to take.

Interviewer's question	**Interviewee's response**
What topics do you feel strongly about?	Education, computers, wildlife conservation, money
Which topic would you like to discuss?	Saving money
What feelings, attitudes, or beliefs do you have about this topic?	I don't like the fact that stores set the price for things I want to buy—there's no bargaining. I don't like having to wait for sales to pay a decent price for an item. That's why this year, I bought all my holiday gifts online.

Would you buy online again?	Definitely
Why?	I didn't have to drive to the stores or fight the crowds. I found some good bargains. I got to choose exactly what I wanted.
Is there anything you don't like about buying online?	I can't actually see or touch the item, but I can pretty much figure out what the item will be like from its picture.
What would you like to persuade others to believe?	I think buying online makes a lot more sense than going to stores.

An Essay Plan

Title The Joys of Shopping Online

Thesis Online shopping offers many advantages to shoppers.

I. Topic sentence for first body paragraph	I. One benefit of making purchases on the Internet is convenience.
A. Major point	A. easy to do
B. Major point	B. any time of day
C. Major point	C. saves time
II. Topic sentence for second body paragraph	II. Internet shopping provides an extraordinary choice of products.
A. Major point	A. many types of items
B. Major point	B. the "perfect" gift
C. Major point	C. not limited to local stores
III. Topic sentence for third body paragraph	III. Shoppers can get top value for their dollar.
A. Major point	A. products often discounted online
B. Major point	B. easy to compare items and features
C. Major point	C. easy to find lowest price

A Model Essay

THE JOYS OF SHOPPING ONLINE

1 Shopping malls and local stores are not headed for extinction. There is, however, a new, ecologically sound way to shop. Shoppers who want to reduce their dependence on motor vehicles, conserve fuel resources, and reduce pollution can simply turn on their computers, head for the Internet, and make their purchases online. Not only is online shopping kind to the environment, it offers advantages to shoppers.

2 One benefit of making purchases on the Internet is convenience. Without a doubt, a leisurely shopping trip can be a positive social experience. Today's busy people, nonetheless, can benefit from an alternative to the time-consuming shopping excursion. Shopping online gives people the ability to make purchases easily, whenever they find time without having to travel. As long as they have Internet access and a credit card, they can shop anytime, day or night. To make a purchase, all they have to do is type an order and click. The merchandise will arrive at their doorstep within a few days. When shoppers have made their purchases, they can close down their computer with a flick of their finger and get on with other things. Shopping online means not spending time driving to and from stores, walking from store to store, and waiting in line to purchase an item. Few people can resist the ease that online shopping offers.

3 In addition to convenience, Internet shopping provides an extraordinary choice of products. Whatever shoppers want is most likely available somewhere on the Web. Does anyone want a copy of a CD that went out of print a decade ago? Perhaps, someone needs parts for a bicycle or television. Is the

perfect gift for Grandma a lace handkerchief handmade in Italy? Who is interested in hardware or software, electronics, or toys? These items, as well as any book, food, plane or concert ticket, piece of clothing—new or used—and much, much more are offered online. Net shopping means moving beyond the limitations of local stores to select from the widest variety of merchandise. Online shopping provides the opportunity to satisfy the desires of every heart.

4 Most important, shoppers can get top value for their dollar on the Web. Products are often discounted because selling online involves fewer overhead costs than selling in a retail store. In addition, before purchasing an item, a person can easily and quickly assess the merits of various models as well as compare items, feature by feature. There are chat rooms where prospective buyers can learn more about what they are purchasing. Online shoppers can compare prices from site to site or at a single site that lists the current best prices for competitive brands. Upon compiling their information, shoppers know that they are buying at the lowest price around. The Internet even provides auction sites where savvy online shoppers offer low bids for goods they want. Given the cost advantages of shopping online, buyers have the satisfaction of spending their hard-earned money wisely.

5 Thank goodness for a wonderful new way to shop. Not only is shopping online convenient, the availability of merchandise is unsurpassed, and the prices are the best anywhere. As a bonus, those who shop online are doing their part to limit vehicle traffic in their community and contribute to the environment. Certainly, traditional stores will not disappear in the near future, but as more people learn about the advantages of shopping online, they, too, will want to point and click to make their purchases.

Here are an interview, plan, and essay persuading readers that shopping online has drawbacks.

Interviewer's question	Interviewee's response
What topics do you feel strongly about?	Education, computers, wildlife conservation, money
Which topic would you like to discuss?	Value for my money
What feelings, attitudes, or beliefs do you have about this topic?	It worries me that people are buying things on the Internet instead of in stores.
What is one of your concerns?	When people buy online they're not spending money in the community. That's going to cut back on money we get from sales tax.
What else?	I think stores will go out of business, and that's going to cost people their jobs.
Would you ever buy online?	I doubt it. I like to see or touch what I buy. Also, I don't want to wait for something to arrive in the mail.
What would you like to persuade others to believe?	I think buying online has a lot of risks.

A Second Essay

Title The Drawbacks of Shopping Online

Thesis Shopping online does not benefit the shopper.

I. Topic sentence for first body paragraph	I. Although there may seem to be advantages to shopping anytime, day or night, in the safety of one's home, these advantages are not what they seem.
A. Major point	A. too much time spent shopping
B. Major point	B. problem of impulse buying
C. Major point	C. insecure sites

II. Topic sentence for second body paragraph	II. Those who praise the economy of shopping online have not considered the real costs.
A. Major point	A. virtual, not real merchandise
B. Major point	B. hidden costs of computer
C. Major point	C. postage and handling costs
III. Topic sentence for third body paragraph	III. Promoters of online shopping are missing perhaps the most important point of all, that shopping, at its best, is a social activity.
A. Major point	A. no real people
B. Major point	B. difficult to share
C. Major point	C. no stops for snacks

A Second Model Essay

THE DRAWBACKS OF SHOPPING ONLINE

1 There's a new look in shopping. People who have Internet access can ignore local stores to make purchases online. Unfortunately, when sales taxes no longer support the hometown, the community must make do with less security, beautification, and recreation. In addition, jobs for residents are lost as local businesses carry on with fewer employees or even close. Perhaps, communities could adjust to these losses if shopping online were of benefit to the consumer. Just the opposite, however, is true. Shopping online does not benefit the shopper.

2 Although there may seem to be advantages to shopping anytime, day or night, in the safety of one's home, these advantages are not what they seem. As any seasoned shopper knows, the more time spent in a store, the more purchases are made. With the stores

just a finger tap away, the time spent browsing is potentially unlimited. Only the most disciplined buyer is able to handle the temptations provided by online shopping. In addition, purchasers who believe that Internet shopping is done in a completely secure environment should understand that unless a site is "secure," the opportunity for cyber thieves to steal credit card information abounds. To keep purchases in line, limit shopping time, and keep credit card numbers between customer and merchant, shoppers are wise to shop in their neighborhood markets and malls.

3 Those who praise the economy of shopping online have not considered the real costs. Relying on information and pictures provided on Web sites is unlike actually seeing and touching the product. It is real, not virtual shopping, that allows the consumer to get the most value per dollar. Then, too, where are the savings when start-up and ongoing costs are included? Initially, the online shopper needs a computer and printer (for receipts of purchases). Every month there is a bill for the network provider and maybe for a second phone line. In addition, charges for handling and postage are generally added to purchase prices. When errors occur, merchandise must be sent back for an additional charge. Exchanges or refunds can be granted only when the online site is still available; sites seem to disappear almost at whim. Buyers who want to shop economically should take their business to hometown establishments, not to virtual stores.

4 Finally, promoters of online shopping are missing perhaps the most important point of all—that shopping, at its best, is a social activity. Even if going to the store involves only casual contact with a sales associate and maybe some other customers, life is in better perspective when seen through a wide lens. Best of all can be sharing a shopping experience. Two are better than one at the poking, prodding, and comparing merchandise that lead to satisfying purchases. Then, too, shopping online does

not provide a food court. At most, online shopping is a solitary, impersonal substitute for the joy of sharing human companionship in real-life/real-time markets.

5 Shoppers need not shop online. If they do connect with the Net, not only do they lose in time, money, and even safety, they do not get the best values most inexpensively. The best shopping is done in their hometown, in the stores owned and operated by fellow citizens. When shoppers frequent their local shops, communities don't confront the consequences of reduced revenue and loss of employment and businesses. The best way to face the new look in shopping is to look the other way.

EXERCISE 3 React to a Persuasive Essay

1. From which point of view is each essay written?

____

2. How does the writer of "The Joys of Shopping Online" appeal to emotions?

____

____

____

____

3. What convincing point(s), if any, does "Joys" make? What points are not convincing?

____

____

____

____

4. Why are the paragraphs in "Joys" ordered as they are? Is this order effective?

5. How does the writer of "The Drawbacks of Shopping Online" appeal to emotions?

6. What convincing point(s), if any, does "Drawbacks" make? What points are not convincing?

7. Why are the paragraphs in "Drawbacks" ordered as they are? Is this order effective?

8. Which essay do you find more convincing? Why?

Work on Writing Assignment 10

EXERCISE 4 Prewrite, Plan, and Draft

Part A

Conduct an interview with a classmate to discuss a subject. Then have the classmate interview you about your subject. Take notes.

Part B

Write an outline for your persuasive essay.

Part C

Use your outline plan to write a draft of your essay. Give your essay a title.

Building Language Skills

Vocabulary

Word Meanings

EXERCISE 5 Use the Dictionary

Write dictionary definitions of the word *mosaic*.

Underline the definition of the word as it is used in the following sentence:

"Within this **mosaic** there is a universal refrain: 'I am so busy.'"

Synonyms

EXERCISE 6 Use the Thesaurus

Explain how the meaning of the phrase changes with the use of each synonym.

"We miss the quiet that gives us **wisdom**."

1. . . . that gives us **wisdom** ______________________________
2. . . . that gives us **intelligence** ______________________________
3. . . . that gives us **insight** ______________________________
4. . . . that gives us **information** ______________________________

Consistency

Musical harmony is a result of a pleasing combination of parts; consistency in writing is similar to musical harmony. In both there are internal agreement and compatibility. Without this harmony in writing, readers are confused and communication is unclear. Good writing requires paying attention to the consistency within various parts of the composition.

What is consistency of verb tense?

To be in harmony, verbs need to be in the same tense unless there is a need to change, as in a flashback.

Correct

present tense ↓ present tense ↓

When we keep the Sabbath, we are using time wisely.

Unintended shifts or changes in verb tense either create nonsense or change the meaning of the sentence.

Incorrect

↓ ↓

When a *past tense* shifts to *present tense,* the meaning is unclear.

When we kept the Sabbath, we are using time wisely.

What is consistency of person?

When you begin writing using "I" and the pronouns related to "I," you continue focusing on "I." Likewise, if you are using "you," you stay with "you." And, if you use the singular and plural forms of "he," "she," and "it," you do not shift to another person.

Correct

The busier **we** are, the more important **we** seem to **ourselves** and, **we** imagine, to others.

Incorrect

The busier **you** are, the more important we seem to ourselves and, we imagine, to others.

What is consistency in number?

"Number" refers to singular and plural. When you start writing in the singular, don't switch to the plural without a reason. When you start writing in the plural, don't switch to the singular without a reason.

Correct

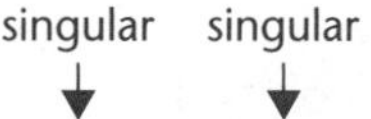

Speak to the **child** of his/**her** hopes and dreams.

Or, less awkward,

Speak to the **children** of their hopes and dreams.

Incorrect

Speak to the **child** of **their** hopes and dreams.

It important to the meaning of a sentence that all the words related to a singular noun are singular and all the words related to a plural noun are plural.

EXERCISE 7 Revise to Avoid Shifts

Revise the following italicized words to make them structurally consistent.

EXAMPLE

Sabbath time is a revolutionary challenge to the violence of overwork because it *honored* the necessity of dormancy.

honors

1. The Sabbath has proven *their* wisdom over the ages.

   ____

2. When we are in the world with *your* eyes open, the seductions are insatiable.

   ____

3. Because we do not rest, we *lost* our way.

   ____

4. We miss the quiet that gives *you* freedom.

   ____

5. We missed the compass points that *will show* us where to go.

   ____

6. Many of *us* feel terrible guilt when *it takes* time to rest.

   ____

7. The Sabbath gives *them* permission to stop to restore our souls.

   ____

Sentence Style

EXERCISE 8 Rearrange Sentences

Rewrite each sentence using the indicated new beginning. Be sure to keep the meaning of the original sentence. Consider the effect of rearranging the words.

1. Many of us, in our desperate drive to be successful and care for our many responsibilities, feel terrible guilt when we take time to rest.

   *Because we have a desperate drive*__________________________

2. The Sabbath has proven its wisdom over the ages.

   Over the ages __________________________________

3. Those quiet Sunday afternoons are embedded in our cultural memory.

   Embedded in our cultural memory __________________________

4. Every responsibility and every stimulus compete for our attention.

   Competing for our attention ____________________________

EXERCISE 9 Combine Sentences

Combine the ideas from the sentences in each group to write one new sentence. As you write each sentence, consider the emphasis and relationships you want to achieve.

1.

We miss the compass points.

The compass points show us something.

They show us where to go.

____

____

____

2.

Many of us still recall something.

We recall when shops were closed on Sundays.

We recall when offices were closed on Sundays.

____

____

____

3.

We can change society.

We can begin a quiet revolution of change.

We can begin it in ourselves.

We can begin it in our families.

____

____

____

4.

The Sabbath gives us permission to do something.

It gives us the permission we need to stop.

It gives us the permission we need to restore ourselves.

____

____

____

Revising the Essay

EXERCISE 10 Rework for Content, Structure, Language, and Accuracy

Part A

1. Is your point of view consistent throughout the essay?
2. Does your organization follow persuasive order?

Revise as needed

Part B

1. Circle two different words that can be made more specific. Write in the margin, near each circled word, the new word. Decide whether to use the original word or its synonym.
2. Highlight one sentence that can be enhanced by rearranging words. Rewrite the new sentence at the bottom of your paper.
3. Highlight two sentences that can be made more effective by combining them. Rewrite the new sentence at the bottom of your paper.

Part C

Proofread your paper to correct misspelled words, typographical errors, and missing words. Using the revisions you made on your draft, type a final copy of your essay.

PART THREE

Language Supplement

The Language Supplement is intended to provide you with some additional background and practice in usage and mechanics. You may want to read it from beginning to end for an overview of some issues to consider as you revise sentences in your papers. It also serves as a reference for finding answers to questions about language as they arise. The practice exercises can help you master the skills you need for effective college and professional writing.

PARTS OF SPEECH

In English, words are divided into eight categories based on the way they function in a sentence. These eight categories, called **parts of speech,** are nouns, pronouns, verbs, adjectives, adverbs, prepositions, conjunctions, and interjections. As you study the parts of speech, it is important to realize that a word may be included in several classifications. The word *house*, for instance, is typically classified as a noun. However, in the sentence "Give some plant food to the house plants," the word *house* functions as an adjective, and in the sentence, "The campers housed their belongings in a shed," the word *house* functions as a verb in the past tense.

Nouns

Definition

A **noun** is a word used as the name of a person, place, thing, or idea.

Kinds

A **proper noun** is the name of a particular person, place, or thing.

Erik, Karin, Brooklyn, Declaration of Independence

A **common noun** is the name of any person, place, thing, or idea.

friend, office, investigation, generosity, health

A **concrete noun** is the name of a person, place, or thing that exists in space.

friend, office, lawn

An **abstract noun** is the name of an idea, quality, or condition that does not occupy space.

love, kindness, perception, generosity

A **collective noun** is the name of a group of persons or things considered as one unit.

class, crowd, mob

Properties

Gender is the property of nouns that indicates masculine or feminine or neuter.

The masculine gender indicates the male sex.

uncle, actor, goose, rooster

The feminine gender indicates the female sex.

aunt, actress, gander, hen

The neuter gender indicates objects without gender.

computer, chair, book

All nouns are in the **third person** since they are persons, places, things, or ideas spoken of.

Number is a property that indicates whether a noun names one thing or more than one thing.

Singular names one. Plural names more than one.

The majority of nouns can be changed from singular to plural by adding -s or -es.

table, tables; lock, locks; box, boxes

Some nouns have irregular plural forms.

ox, oxen; foot, feet; tooth, teeth; deer, deer

A few nouns cannot be made plural because they name something that cannot easily be counted.

peace, honesty, dust

Possessive case primarily shows ownership.

John's computer; Carolyn's car; Janice's skis; boys' books; nurse's schedule; nurses' schedule

Pronouns

Definition

A **pronoun** is a word used in place of a noun.

Types	Examples
Personal	I, you, he, she, it, we, they, me, him, her, us, them, my, mine, your, yours, his, her, hers, its, our, ours, their, theirs
Relative	who, whose, whom, which, what, that
Indefinite	all, another, any, anyone, anybody, both, each, either, everyone, few, someone, many, neither, nobody, none, somebody
Interrogative	who? whose? whom? which? what?
Demonstrative	this, that, these, those
Reflexive	myself, yourself, yourselves, himself, herself, itself, ourselves, themselves

Personal pronouns are used to indicate the person speaking, the person spoken to, or the person spoken of.

> **I** say **you** can't hold a man down without staying down with **him**.
>
> — Attributed to Booker T. Washington (1856–1915)

A **relative pronoun** relates to, or is connected with, a noun that precedes it (called an **antecedent.**)

> The nail **that** sticks up will be hammered down.
>
> — Japanese Proverb.

(**Nail** is the antecedent of *that.*)

Anyone **who** has never made a mistake has never tried anything new.

— Albert Einstein (1879–1955)

(**Anyone** is the antecedent of *who.*)

Indefinite pronouns name an object or objects in general. Nouns, verbs, and other pronouns that refer to indefinite pronouns must agree with them in number. The indefinite pronouns that end in *body* or *one* are singular; *each, either, neither* are also singular.

When **everyone** is **somebody**, then **no one** is **anybody**!

— Sir William Gilbert (1836–1911)

Interrogative pronouns are used to ask questions.

What's in a name? That which we call a rose by any other name would smell as sweet.

— William Shakespeare (1546–1616)

Demonstrative pronouns point out which one or which ones.

This is a world of compensations; and he who would be no slave must consent to have no slave. **Those** who deny freedom to others deserve it not for themselves, and under a just God, cannot long retain it.

— Abraham Lincoln (1809–1865)

Reflexive pronouns help to clarify a preceding noun. When they are used for emphasis, they are called **intensive pronouns.**

No man is happy who does not think **himself** so.

— Publilius Syrus (first century B.C.)

If I am not for **myself**, who is for me? And when I am for **myself**, what am I? And if not now, when?

— Hillel (30 B.C.E.–A.D. 10)

The **case of a pronoun** shows the pronoun's relationship to the rest of the sentence. The three cases of pronouns are the nominative, the objective, and the possessive.

Nominative Case	I, you, she, he, we, they, who, whoever
Objective Case	me, you, him, her, us, them, whom, whomever
Possessive Case	my, mine, your, yours, his, her, hers, our, ours, their, theirs, whose

The case of a pronoun depends upon how it is used in a sentence. Notice how the form of ***we*** changes as its use in each sentence changes.

Nominative Case	**We** knew the coach.
Objective Case	The coach knew **us.**
Possessive Case	**Our** coach knew the rules.

Adjectives

Definition

An **adjective** is a word that describes a noun or pronoun.

> The difference between the almost **right** word and the **right** word is really a **large** matter—it's the difference between the **lightning** bug and lightning.
>
> — Samuel Clemens (1835–1910)

Properties

One-syllable adjectives and some two-syllable adjectives add *-er* in comparing two things and *-est* when comparing three or more things. Some two-syllable words and all longer adjectives are compared by adding *more* for two things and *most* for three or more. Negative comparisons are formed with the words *less* and *least.*

> Imagination is **more important** than knowledge.
>
> — Albert Einstein (1879–1955)
>
> He can compress the **most** words into the **smallest** ideas of any man I ever met.
>
> — Abraham Lincoln (1809–1865)

Adverbs

Definition

Adverbs describe verbs, adjectives, or other adverbs. They often end in *-ly.*- Other common adverbs are *not, never, seldom,* and *often.*

> It is remarkable how **easily** and **insensibly** we fall into a particular route and make a beaten track for ourselves.
>
> — Henry David Thoreau (1817–1862)

Properties

Adverbs, like adjectives, are compared using *more* and *most* and *less* and *least.*

> There is no kind of dishonesty into which otherwise good people **more easily** and **frequently** fall than that of defrauding the government.
> — Benjamin Franklin (1706–1790)

Prepositions

Definition

A **preposition** is a word used to show the relation of a noun or pronoun to some other word in the sentence. A preposition is followed by a noun or pronoun object to form a **prepositional phrase.**

Types

Direction	Position		Time	Other
along	above	beside	after	against
down	across	between	at	by
from	against	by	before	except
into	among	in	by	for
over	around	off	during	of
through	at	on	in	with
to	before	under	since	without
toward	behind	upon	until	
up	beneath	within	within	

Sentences may contain one prepositional phrase, or they may contain many prepositional phrases.

> Let there be space **in** your togetherness.
>
> — Kahlil Gibran, *The Prophet* (1923)
>
> **On** the left side **of** the plank, **beyond** the girl, sat a boy **about** seven years old—a well-grown lad, his skin deeply tanned, a certain clever, watchful gleam **in** his eyes. **With** hands folded **over** one knee, he looked straight ahead.
>
> — O.E. Rolvaag, *Giants in the Earth* (1927)

Verbs

Definition

A **verb** is a word that expresses action or helps to make a statement and shows tense or time.

> In the past we **have had** a light which **flickered**, in the present we **have** a light which **flames**, and in the future there **will be** a light which **shines** over all the land and sea.
>
> — Winston Churchill (1874–1965)

Kinds

A **verb phrase** is made up of a main verb and one or more helping verbs.

> **would have known**
>
> **am going**
>
> **will have been asked**

Helping verbs, sometimes called auxiliary verbs, are used to support a main verb.

> **would have** known
>
> **am** going
>
> **will have been** asked

Tense

The time expressed by a verb is its **tense.**
The **present tense** shows an action or state of being occurring now, at the present time.

> I **know** not what course others may **take**, but as for me, **give** me liberty, or **give** me death!
>
> — Patrick Henry (1736–1799)

The **present perfect** tense shows an action begun in the past and either just completed or still going on.

> I **have bought** golden opinions from all sorts of people.
>
> — William Shakespeare, *Macbeth* (1564–1616)

The **past tense** expresses action (or state of being) in the past that did not continue into the present.

> Never in the field of human conflict **was** so much **owed** by so many to so few.
>
> — Winston Churchill (1874–1965)

The **past perfect** tense shows an action finished in the past before another past action was begun.

> Twice or thrice **had** I **loved** thee, before I **knew** thy face or name.
>
> — John Donne (1572–1631)

Future tense shows an action that has not yet taken place.

> Any excuse **will serve** a tyrant.
>
> — Aesop (620–560 B.C.)
>
> He who builds on every man's advice **will have** a crooked house.
>
> — Dutch saying

Voice

The verb is in the **active voice** when the doer of an action is the subject of the sentence.

> An old pipe **gives** the sweetest smoke.
>
> — Irish saying

The verb is in the **passive voice** when the subject is the receiver of the action.

> The sweetest smoke **is given** by an old pipe.
>
> Irish saying

Verbals

The **infinitive**, the main form of a verb, shows no tense. It consists of the word *to* followed by a verb. (If it is not followed by a verb, *to* is a preposition)

> **To weep** is to make less the depth of grief.
>
> — William Shakespeare (1546–1616)

The **gerund** is a verb acting as a noun. It ends in *-ing.*

> **Reading** maketh a full man, conference a reading man, and **writing** an exact man.
>
> — Sir Francis Bacon (1561–1626)

The **participle** is a verb form that modifies a noun or pronoun like an adjective.

> The gray mist of evening, **rising** slowly from the river, enveloped her as she disappeared up the bank, and the **swollen** current and **floundering** masses of ice presented a hopeless barrier between her and her pursuer.
>
> — Harriet Beecher Stowe, *Uncle Tom's Cabin* (1852)
>
> People with **clenched** fists can not shake hands.
>
> — Indira Nehru Gandhi (1917–1984)

Conjunctions

Definition

A **conjunction** is a word that joins two words or two parts of a sentence.

Kinds

Coordinating conjunctions connect words, phrases, or clauses of equal rank. They are *and, but, for, nor, or, so, yet.*

> Where there is charity **and** wisdom, there is neither fear **nor** ignorance.
>
> — Saint Francis of Assisi (c. 1181–1226)
>
> The flow of the river is ceaseless, **and** its water is never the same.
>
> — Kamo no Chomei (1153–1216)

Subordinating conjunctions connect clauses of unequal rank. They introduce dependent clauses.

> **If** we had no winter, the spring would not be so pleasant; **if** we did not sometimes taste adversity, prosperity would not be so welcome.
>
> — Anne Bradstreet (c. 1612–1672)

Correlative conjunctions connect words, phrases, or clauses of the same rank. They are used in pairs. The principal ones are *both . . . and*, *either . . . or*, *neither . . . nor*, *not only . . . but also*.

Where there is peace and meditation, there is **neither** anxiety **nor** doubt.
— Saint Francis of Assisi (c. 1181–1226)

We secure our friends **not by** accepting favors **but by** doing them.
— Thucydides (c. 460–400 B.C.)

Interjections

Definition

An interjection expresses strong feeling.

And when I feigned an angry look,
Alas! I loved you best.
— John Sheffield (1648–1721)

Oh, how fine it is to know a thing or two.
— Jean Baptiste Poquelin Molière (1622–1673)

AGREEMENT

Agreement of Subject and Verb

Definition

A verb is either singular or plural to match its subject.

When a singular word is used as a subject, the verb is singular. Notice that singular verbs end in "s."

Character **is** habit long continued.

— Greek saying

A fool **says** what he **knows**; a wise man **knows** what he **says**.

— Yiddish saying

When a plural word is used as a subject, the verb is plural.

The cruelest lies **are** often told in silence.

— Robert Louis Stevenson (1850–1894)

Locate the subject before deciding if the verb is singular or plural.

The subject of a sentence is not in a prepositional phrase.

The most common **trait** of all primitive peoples **is** a reverence for the life-giving earth.

— Stewart Lee Udall (1920–1963)

The subject may come after the verb.

Between the idea and the reality **falls** the **shadow**.

— T. S. Eliot (1888–1965)

These **are** the **times** that try men's souls.

— Thomas Paine (1736–1809)

The words *there* and *here* are **never** the subject of a sentence.

There **is** advantage in the wisdom won from pain.

— Æschylus (525–456 B.C.)

There **are** no menial jobs, only menial attitudes.

— William John Bennett (1943–)

EXERCISE 1 Subject/Verb Agreement

In each sentence, underline the subject. If the subject is singular, write S on the line before the sentence. If the subject is plural, write P on the line. Then, underline the verb that correctly completes the sentence.

Example

__P__ Many *people* from countries all over the world (visit, visits) the Statue of Liberty each year.

1. ______ The people of France (was, were) proud to give the American people the Statue of Liberty that now stands in New York Harbor.

2. ______ Designed by French sculptor Frederic Auguste Bartholdi, the Statue (depict, depicts) political freedom.

3. ______ The Statue, weighing 450,000 pounds, or 225 tons, (has, have) an additional 200,000 pounds of copper sheeting.

4. ______ The 167 steps from ground level to the top of the pedestal, the 168 steps inside the Statue to the head, and the 54 rungs on the ladder to the arm that holds the torch (are, is) part of the original design.

5. ______ Dedicated on October 28, 1886, the Statue of Liberty now (has, have) designation as a national monument.

6. ______ For the centennial celebrations on July 4, 1986, the Statue (was, were) extensively restored.

7. ______ The Statue of Liberty, which symbolizes liberty in the form of a woman, (has, have) been called "Liberty Enlightening the World."

8. ______ Lady Liberty (holds, hold) a torch high in her right hand and (carries, carry) in her left hand a book of law inscribed "July 4, 1776."

9. ______ Broken chains that symbolize the overthrow of tyranny (lie, lies) at her feet.

10. ______ As travelers sail into New York Harbor, one of the first sights they see (is, are) this magnificent Lady.

EXERCISE 2 Subject/Verb Agreement

In each sentence, if the verb agrees with its subject, write "correct" on the line before the sentence. If a verb is incorrect, underline the verb and write the correct form of the verb on the line.

1. ______ Ellis Island was incorporated as part of the Statue of Liberty National Monument on May 11, 1965.

2. ______ The facilities on Ellis Island was in use from 1892 to 1954.

3. ______ During that time, about 12 million immigrants coming to the United States as steerage or third-class steamship passengers were inspected at Ellis Island.

4. ______ Each of these passengers were examined for legal and medical acceptability.
5. ______ Today, millions of Americans is descended from immigrants that arrived in the United States through Ellis Island.
6. ______ Following major reconstruction, the main building was reopened on September 10, 1990.
7. ______ This building, used for processing immigrants, were restored as part of the centennial celebration in 1992.
8. ______ A part of the celebration activities was the opening of the Ellis Island Immigration Museum.
9. ______ Visitors to the three-floor museum becomes aware of the difficult experiences faced by those who left their homelands for America.
10. ______ A tourist taking time to see the restored sections of the building and the educational display has learned something about an important part of American history.

Agreement of Pronoun and Antecedent

Definition

An antecedent is a word or word group to which a pronoun refers. A pronoun agrees in number with its antecedent.

Locate the antecedent before deciding whether to use a singular or plural pronoun.

When an antecedent is singular, the pronoun is singular.

> If **money** be not thy servant, **it** will be thy master. The covetous **man** cannot so properly be said to possess wealth, as that may be said to possess **him**.
>
> — Sir Francis Bacon (1561–1626)
>
> A **mother** never realizes that **her** children are no longer children.
>
> — James Agee (1909–1955)
>
> When I was a young man I vowed never to marry until I found the ideal **woman**. Well, I found **her** but, alas, **she** was waiting for the ideal man.
>
> — Anonymous

When an antecedent is plural, the pronoun is plural.

In the case of good **books**, the point is not to see how many of **them** you can get through, but how many can get through to you.

— Mortimer Adler (1902–)

Words, once **they** are printed, have a life of **their** own.

— Carol Burnett (1933–)

Use a singular pronoun to refer to indefinite pronouns, such as anyone, anybody, everybody.

Anybody who has **her** wits about **her** knows that two plus two is sometimes five.

— Anonymous

Nothing happens to **anybody** which **he** is not fitted by nature to bear.

— Marcus Aurelius Antoninus (121–180)

Nobody, as long as **he** moves about among the currents of life, is without trouble.

— Carl Gustav Jung (1875–1961)

Use a plural pronoun when two or more antecedents are joined by "and."

Both tears **and** sweat are salty, but **they** render a different result. Tears will get you sympathy; sweat will get you change.

— Jesse Jackson (1941–)

Use a singular pronoun when two or more antecedents are joined by "or" or "nor."

Neither a wise man **nor** a brave man lies down on the tracks of history to wait for the train of the future to run over **him**.

— Dwight David Eisenhower (1890–1969)

Use either a singular or a plural pronoun with a collective noun depending on whether the collective noun is used in a singular or plural sense.

You don't choose your **family**. **They** are God's gift to you, as you are to **them**.

— Desmond Tutu (1931–)

All happy families resemble one another, but each unhappy **family** is unhappy in **its** own way.

— Leo Tolstoy (1828–1910)

EXERCISE 3 Pronoun Agreement

In the following sentences, choose the correct pronoun and write its antecedent on the line before the sentence.

1 _______ The Hare liked to make fun of the Tortoise because (he, they) moved exceedingly slowly.

2. _______ Finally, the Tortoise, tired of the Hare's taunting, suggested that a race take place between the Hare and (him, them).

3. _______ Gathering to watch the race, the other animals believed the Tortoise, the slowest of (him, them) all, had no chance of beating the Hare.

4. _______ At the starting signal, the Hare bounded down the road, and soon (he, they) was far ahead of the slow-moving Tortoise.

5. _______ When he could no longer see the Tortoise behind him, the Hare thought to himself, "I agree with all the animals. Of course, (I, they) will easily win this race."

6. _______ The Hare decided to rest for a while under the leafy trees and was soon fast asleep in (its, their) shade.

7. _______ Meanwhile, the Tortoise, trudging inch by inch down the hot, dusty road, passed (his, their) opponent, the Hare, napping comfortably.

8. _______ Without taking a break for (himself, themselves), the Tortoise plodded on towards the goal.

9. _______ When the Hare woke up with a start, he saw the Tortoise crossing the finish line far ahead, and he could hear all the animals cheering (its, their) winner.

10. _______ Slow and steady, the Tortoise had proven (his, their) strength.

11. _______ Each of Aesop's fables has (its, their) lesson for humanity.

EXERCISE 4 Pronoun Agreement

For each sentence, if each pronoun agrees with its antecedent, write "correct" on the line before the sentence. If a pronoun is incorrect, underline the pronoun and write the correct pronoun on the line.

Example

__*his*__ Late one night a mysterious stranger granted King Midas <u>her</u> wish that everything he touched should turn to gold.

1. ______ Walking in his garden in the morning, the king happily turned some red roses and even the worms inside its petals into solid gold.

2. ______ As he sat at breakfast, however, he was astonished to hear his beloved daughter sobbing and to see him carrying into the room one of the golden roses.

3. ______ The girl said, through their tears, that when she had gone to gather him some beautiful red roses, all she had found were sharp, unscented gold stems.

4. ______ Then to the King's shocked amazement, everything on the breakfast table turned to gold at its touch—the dishes, the spoons and forks, and his food.

5. ______ Distressed by her father's alarm, the daughter ran to hug him, and, of course, immediately she turned to gold.

6. ______ Looking at the golden statue that had been their warm and caring daughter, King Midas prayed to be rid of their golden touch.

7. ______ When the stranger reappeared, the King pleaded with them to take back the gift of gold.

8. ______ To be free, the King had to bathe in the river and then sprinkle water on whatever they no longer wanted gold.

9. ______ Hugging his daughter, brought back to life, King Midas knew that for him gold was no longer the most important part of your life.

PUNCTUATION

Punctuation helps express clear written thought. The importance of punctuation can be illustrated by the following sentences. Notice the change that punctuation makes in meaning.

> The rooster strutted and squawked an hour after his head was cut off.
>
> The rooster strutted and squawked. An hour after, his head was cut off.

Punctuation Rule	*Examples*
	COMMA
Use a comma to separate *words* in a series.	In the realm of Nature, there is nothing purposeless, trivial, or unnecessary. — Maimonides (1135–1204)
Use a comma to separate *phrases* in a series.	To marry once is duty, twice a folly, but thrice is madness. — Dutch saying
Use a comma to separate *clauses* in a series	I came, I saw, and I conquered. — Julius Caesar (100–44 B.C.)
Use a comma to separate a *word* preceding the subject of a sentence from the rest of the sentence.	Peace, it is peace that must guide the destinies of peoples and of all mankind. — Pope Paul VI (1897–1978)
Use a comma to separate a *phrase* preceding the subject of a sentence from the rest of the sentence.	To me, party platforms are contracts with the people. — Harry S. Truman (1884–1972)
	On the breast of her gown, in fine red cloth, surrounded with elaborate embroidery and fantastic flourishes of gold thread, appeared the letter A. — Nathaniel Hawthorne, *The Scarlet Letter* (1850)
Use a comma to separate *a clause* preceding the subject of a sentence from the rest of the sentence.	As he thinks in his heart, so is he. — Proverbs 23:7
	If we wait for the moment when everything, absolutely everything, is ready, we shall never begin. — Ivan Turgenev (1818–1883)

Use a comma to set off a noun in *apposition,* a noun that renames what has come before.

I traveled in the care of a mountain boy, Jake Marpole, one of the "hands" on my father's old farm under the Blue Ridge.

— Willa Cather, *My Antonia* (1918)

Use a comma to separate a short direct quotation from the rest of the sentence.

"Did you ever think you might run yourself, Jim?" he asked.

— Stephen Crane, *The Red Badge of Courage* (1895)

"Surely," thought Rip, "I have not slept here all night."

— Washington Irving, *Rip Van Winkle* (1819)

Use a comma to separate parenthetical expressions from the rest of the sentence.

A great writer is, so to speak, a second government in his county.

— Alexander Isayeevich Solzhenitsyn (1918–)

Money, it is said, is the root of all evil.

— Folk Saying

Use a comma to separate a nonrestrictive clause from the word it modifies. (A nonrestrictive clause is one that does not limit the meaning or add anything important to the idea of the sentence.)

My father, who was very ancient, had given me a competent share of learning, as far as house-education and a country free school generally goes.

— Daniel Defoe, *Robinson Crusoe* (1719)

Use a comma to separate clauses joined by *and, but, for, so, yet,* and *or.*

The young man who has not wept is a savage**, and** the old man who will not laugh is a fool.

— George Santayana (1863–1952)

	My feet are tired**, but** my soul is rested. — Rosa Parks (1913–1955)
	I cannot and will not recant anything**, for** to go against conscience is neither right nor safe. — Martin Luther Jr. (1483–1546)
	I like to hear rain on a tin roof**, so** I covered part of my roof with tin. — Samuel Clemens (1835–1910)
	She speaks**, yet** she says nothing. — William Shakespeare (1564–1616)
	Mankind must put an end to war**, or** war will put an end to mankind. — John F. Kennedy (1917–1963)
Use commas to separate the parts of a date.	By Tuesday**,** January 15**,** 2006**,** the project must be completed.
Use commas to separate the parts of an address.	Write to Naomi at 810 Michigan Avenue**,** Chicago**,** Illinois.

Punctuation Rule	***Examples***

SEMICOLON

Use a semicolon to separate the clauses of a compound sentence when there is no conjunction.	I will not steep my speech in lies**;** the test of any man lies in action. — Pindar (c. 518–438 B.C.)

You have seen how a man was made a slave; you shall see how a slave was made a man.

— Frederick Douglass (1817–1895)

Use a semicolon to separate the parts of a compound sentence when these parts have commas within themselves.

If left to himself, he would have whistled life away in perfect contentment; but his wife kept continually dinning in his ears about his idleness, his carelessness, and the ruin he was bringing on his family.

— Washington Irving, *Rip Van Winkle* (1819)

Use a semicolon between clauses of a compound sentence that are joined by *therefore, hence, however, nevertheless, moreover, accordingly, besides, also, thus, then, still,* and *otherwise.*

I think; therefore, I am.

— René Descartes (1596–1650)

COLON

Use a colon to separate a long quotation or a list from the rest of the sentence.

There are two ways of spreading light: to be the candle or the mirror that reflects it.

— Edith Wharton (1862–1937)

PARENTHESES

Use parentheses to enclose a remark that might be omitted without altering the sense of the sentence.

It is a little village of great antiquity, having been founded by some of the Dutch colonists, in the early times of the province, just about the beginning of the government of the good Peter Stuyvesant (may he rest in peace!).

— Washington Irving, *Rip Van Winkle* (1819)

DASH

Use a dash as a substitute for parentheses to indicate something added to the sentence without being necessary to its meaning.

A man does what he must—in spite of personal consequences, in spite of obstacles and dangers and pressures—and that is the basis of all human morality

— John F. Kennedy, *Profiles in Courage* (1956)

APOSTROPHE

Use an apostrophe and an "s" to indicate the possessive case for nouns.

A scholar's ink lasts longer than a martyr's blood.

— Irish saying

Use an apostrophe to indicate the omission of a letter or letters.

That's one small step for man, one giant leap for mankind.

— Neil Armstrong, July 20, 1969

Use an apostrophe to show possession and to form the plural of numbers and letters and words considered as words.

A man's character is his fate.
— Heraclitus (c. 540–480 B.C.)

Mind your p's and q's.
— American saying

QUOTATION MARKS

Use quotation marks to enclose the exact words of a speaker or writer. Periods and commas are always placed inside quotation marks.

"The trial cannot proceed," said the King, in a very grave voice, "until all the jurymen are back in their proper places."
"If everybody minded his own business," the Duchess said in a hoarse growl, "the world would go round a deal faster than it does."
The King said, "Let the jury consider their verdict."

	"Off with her head!" the Queen shouted at the top of her voice. "Who cares for you?" said Alice. "You're nothing but a pack of cards." — Lewis Carroll, *Alice's Adventures in Wonderland* (1865)
Use quotation marks to enclose a quoted title. Note: A quotation within a quotation is set off by single quotation marks.	Tennyson wrote "The Idylls of the King." Shakespeare is called "The Bard of Avon." Raphael's "Sistine Madonna" is a world famous painting. "Breathes there a man with soul so dead Who never to himself hath said, 'This is my own, my native land'." — Sir Walter Scott (1771–1832)
Use quotation marks to indicate a word itself, not its meaning.	Define "onomatopoeia." You must dot your "i's" and cross your "t's."

EXERCISE 5 Commas

Read the following sentences to determine if commas are needed at the ^ marks. If so, add them.

1. Baseball ^ although it was quite different from the game of today ^ was played during the early 1800s in the northeastern United States.

2. Variations of the game were known even earlier in the United States ^ in England ^ and in other areas.

3. According to the Baseball Hall of Fame ^ a newspaper in Delaware ^ County ^ in New York State on July 13 ^ 1825 ^ posted an announcement seeking nine men to play a game of baseball.

4 Popular belief is that Abner Doubleday ^ the officially recognized creator of baseball ^ invented the game in Cooperstown ^ New York ^ in 1839.

5. It may be that the rules for the game were first adopted in September ^ 1845 ^ by a team known as the New York Knickerbockers.

6. The Knickerbockers played in the first organized baseball game ^ using the new rules in June ^ 1846 ^ in Hoboken ^ New Jersey.

7. During the Civil War ^ Union soldiers taught the game ^ to men in other parts of the country.

8. As its popularity increased ^ the game became more expensive ^ so spectators were charged admission ^ and teams had to find sponsors and ask for donations.

9. In 1871 ^ the National Association became the first professional baseball league.

10. Professional teams increased the popularity of the sport into the twentieth century ^ and old timers today may remember ^ when they traded baseball cards and listened to the World Series over a speaker system in their classrooms.

EXERCISE 6 Commas

Add commas as needed. Be able to tell why you added a comma.

1. To honor the Olympian god Zeus a foot race was held at a sacred place in Olympia Peloponnese in 776 B.C.

2. The games at Olympia developed into a truly fabulous festival with a variety of activities for participating athletes.

3. Thousands of athletes and spectators attended the Olympic Festival which took place every fourth summer

4. Some of the early activities included wrestling boxing equestrian events and the pentathlon (jumping running javelin discus and wrestling).

5. The winners of the various events received congratulations an olive branch and rewards from their home city.

6. In 394 A.D. when a Roman emperor conquered Greece the games were cancelled and most of the festival site in Olympia was destroyed.

7. Early in the nineteenth century the Olympic games were reestablished by Greek people wanting to reconnect with their heritage.

8. The games became international with the first summer competition in Athens Greece in 1896 and the first winter competition in Chamonix France in 1924.

9. Since they were reintroduced the games have been held every four years except for 1916 1940 and 1944.

10. The Olympic Games because of a schedule change are now held every two years with winter and summer games alternating so that winter games will be held in 2002 2006 and 2010 and summer games will be held in 2000 2004 and 2008.

EXERCISE 7 Apostrophes

Add apostrophes as needed at the ^ marks. Circle any apostrophes you add.

1. Cunard Line ^ s *Queen Elizabeth 2* was built at John Brown ^ s Harbor on the Clyde in Scotland

2. The *Queen Elizabeth 2* ^ s maiden voyage was ^ in 1969.

3. Fondly known as the *QE2*, she is one of the sea ^ s largest and fastest passenger ship ^ s.

4. With a top speed of 32.5 knots, the *QE2* weighs 70,327 tons ^ , and she ^ s 963 feet long.

5. A luxury ocean liner, the *QE2* cruises ^ around the world every year from January to April; afterwards, she ^ s occupied making crossings between New York and England.

6. Accommodating 1,900 passengers, the *QE2* maintain ^ s a crew of 1,015.

7. In 1987 the *QE2* ^ s engines were converted from steam to diesel.

8. It wasn ^ t until July 1990 that this ocean liners ^ time crossing the Atlantic from Southampton, England, to New York was reduced to just over 105 hours.

9. She ^ s been at sea for 30 years, and she ^ s traveled more than 4.25 million nautical miles.

10. There are probably many people who would enjoy a trip around the world in a ship featuring five restaurants ^ and two café ^ s, three swimming pools ^, a cinema, casino, shopping promenade, health club, beauty salon, library, and a computer learning center.

EXERCISE 8 Apostrophes

Add apostrophes as needed. Circle the apostrophes you add. Be prepared to explain the use of each added apostrophe.

1. Britains and Frances aerospace corporations cooperated to build the Concorde, a supersonic airplane.

2. The Concorde made its maiden flight in 1969.

3. To improve pilots vision in taking off and landing, the planes nose can be tilted down by 12.5 degrees.

4. The 31,569 gallons of fuel in its tanks arent just used for flying—theyre also used to balance the plane.

5. The Concordes take-off speed is 250 mph, its cruising speed is 1,336 mph, and its landing speed is 187 mph.

6. As the jet flies at supersonic speeds, wind friction causes the planes outer shell to heat up to 260 degrees Farenheit.

7. Because of the four jet engines noise, the Concorde can fly at its highest speeds only over water.

8. Despite the Concordes expensive body and extravagant fuel needs, it seats only 144 passengers.

9. The super fast planes limitations have resulted in only 16 Concordes ever being sold.

10. Today, new supersonic passenger jets are being planned as part of NASAs High-Speed Research Program, involving Americas major aerospace companies.

EXERCISE 9 Quotation Marks

Punctuate and capitalize in each of the following sentences as needed.

1. As they left zoology class, Becca said to Rob and Bridgette emperor penguins are certainly handsome. They look like they are wearing tuxedos, ready for a fancy party.

2. Rob added they are quite large. They often stand almost four feet tall and weigh up to 90 pounds.

3. Did you realize that no one knows where they go for the summer? asked Becca.

4. I didn't know answered Rob but I do know that the emperor penguins are the only species to reproduce in the winter.

5. Rob said that the female lays only one egg.

6. After she lays the egg, she goes off for two months while the male tends the egg added Becca.

7. She's not totally irresponsible though Becca continued since she returns to feed and care for the penguin chick.

8. On a different topic, Rob said, penguins don't fly. They slide over land on their stomachs.

9. Becca said that the penguins eat small fish, and the sharks eat the penguins.

10. Well said Becca I, for one, would like to see them as they gather on the shores of the Antarctica Sea.

EXERCISE 10 Quotation Marks

Punctuate and capitalize each of the following sentences as needed.

1. Rob asked have you ever seen a hummingbird?

2. Yes, replied Becca. They can be as small as two inches and as large as eight inches.

3. Rob said there are almost 350 different kinds of hummingbirds, and some have red or green metallic throats.

4. He continued explaining that they hover in the air almost motionless with their wings beating between 38 and 78 times a second.

5. Don't be fooled that they will stay in any one place, said Becca, for they can suddenly dart off in any direction at up to 60 miles an hour.

6. Rob said you can find hummingbirds only in the Western Hemisphere, anywhere from southern Alaska to the tip of Cape Horn.

7. Did you know these birds migrate all the way to South America from as far north as Alaska? asked Becca.

8. She added they do eat the equivalent of half their body weight in nectar or sugar every day.

9. They suck up their food through their hollow, straw-like tongues, Rob said.

10. Rob announced I have to get to work now, Becca. See you Friday in class.

CAPITALIZATION

Capitalization is a form of emphasis.

Capitalization Rule	*Examples*
Capitalize the first word of every sentence.	**T**he more beautiful and charming were the smiles of nature, the more horrible and desolate was my condition. **I** saw nothing without seeing it, and I heard nothing without hearing it. — Frederick Douglass (1817–1895), *My Bondage and My Freedom*
Capitalize the names of days of the week, months of the year, and holidays. (Do not capitalize the seasons.)	**T**uesday, **A**pril, **T**hanksgiving, fall, winter, summer, spring
Capitalize all proper nouns and adjectives.	**F**rench, **I**talian, **S**panish, **P**ortuguese, **C**hinese, **C**hristian, **J**ewish, **M**uslim
Capitalize titles of honor and respect, when such titles are part of a name.	The soldiers saluted **G**eneral **W**ashington.
Capitalize the names of points of the compass when they indicate a section of the country.	The words of Henry Clay, "I know no **N**orth, **S**outh, or **E**ast, or **W**est," should express the sentiments of every American.
Capitalize the first word and all important words in a title.	Nathaniel Hawthorne wrote ***T**he **S**carlet **L**etter* and ***T**he **H**ouse of **S**even **G**ables*.

Capitalize the first word of a direct quotation.	Nathan Hale's last words were "**M**y only regret is that I have but one life to give for my country."
Capitalize abbreviations of titles, degrees or honors written after an individual's name.	Albert Einstein, **Ph.D.,** devised the theory of relativity. Thanks to Jonas Salk, **M.D.,** we have the polio vaccine.
Capitalize the name of anything personified.	The **S**un now rose upon the left, Out of the sea came he. Under the onslaught of the barbarians, Civilization reeled and fell.
Capitalize the first word of every line of poetry.	**Y**es, I answered you last night; **N**o, this morning, Sir, I say: **C**olors seen by candlelight **W**ill not look the same by day. — Elizabeth Barrett Browning, *The Lady's Yes* (1844)
Capitalize the pronoun "I" and the interjection "O."	**O** Captain! My captain! Our fearful trip is done. — Walt Whitman (1819–1892)
Capitalize every name or title of the deity and every pronoun referring to the deity.	"We praise **T**hee, O **G**od; we acknowledge **T**hee to be the **L**ord" are the opening words of an old hymn.

EXERCISE 11 Capitalization

Add capital letters as necessary in the following sentences.

1. An important american writer of the nineteenth century is samuel langhorne clemens, known as mark twain.

2. When samuel clemens was four, he moved from florida, missouri, to hannibal, missouri, on the mississippi river.

3. Working as a steamboat pilot on the mississippi river just before the civil war provided him an education in river life.

4. When he left the river to become a newspaper reporter in virginia city, nevada, clemens began signing his name as mark twain.

5. Riverboat workers used the call "mark twain" to indicate that the water was two fathoms deep.

6. One of twain's stories, "the celebrated jumping frog of calaveras county," was popular throughout the nation.

7. Other well-known works of mark twain include 'the adventures of tom sawyer" and "the adventures of huckleberry finn."

8. A person who earns a b.a. degree in american literature will almost certainly read stories by mr. samuel clemens.

EXERCISE 12 Commas

Capitalize words as necessary in the following sentences.

1. Jazz, first played by solo pianists and small bands, is one of the few forms of music developed in the united states.

2. This music evolved from west african music, black american folk music, and european popular and classical music.

3. Jazz had its beginnings in the early 1900s in new orleans, louisiana.

4. Louis armstrong was largely responsible for establishing jazz as an american institution.

5. Known for his ability to improvise, armstrong freely changed popular tunes and lyrics.

6. With a variety of nicknames, such as satchmo and pops, armstrong traveled throughout the world as an unofficial music ambassador for the united states.

7. After his death in the early 1970s, he was posthumously awarded a grammy lifetime achievement award and two hall of fame grammy awards.

8. From new orleans, jazz grew in popularity in chicago, harlem, kansas city, and later on the west coast.

9. Trumpeter wynton marsalis, during the1980s, created a new interest in jazz.

10. In addition to courses in french, english, math and economics, many colleges offer a course in the history of american jazz.

HOMONYMS AND WORD PAIRS

Homonyms and word pairs sound alike, or nearly alike, but have different meanings.

advice, advise

Advise means "to give information or advice."

A*dvice* means "information" or "guidance."

> Career counselors *advise* their clients about finding a job.
>
> The *advice* the counselors give about writing resumes is useful.

affect, effect

Affect means "to influence."

Effect means "result."

> Well-written resumes *affect* potential employers positively.
>
> Well-written resumes have a positive *effect* on potential employers.

have, of

Have is often used in the phrases "could *have*," "might *have*," or "would *have*."

Of shows relationship, as in the "the pages *of* the book."

> Dressing appropriately for the interview *might have* won the applicant the job.
>
> Successful job applicants know which *of* their outfits are appropriate for interviews.

its, it's

It's means "it is."

"Its" means "belonging to it."

> *It's* the early bird that catches the worm.
>
> The early bird has *its* breakfast early.

loose, lose

Loose means "free, not fastened."

Lose means "to part with accidentally."

> The human resources department managers *lose* no time in hiring additional staff.
>
> Twenty applications were lying *loose* on the desk.

quiet, quite

Quiet means "silent."

Q*uite* means "completely."

> Some people are *quiet* when they receive good news.
>
> Some people become *quite* boisterous when they hear positive information.

than, then

Than joins two parts of a comparison.

Then means "at that time."

Thinking about having to do something is often more tiring *than* actually doing it.

When the applications are complete, *then* mail them.

their, they're, there

Their (belonging to them) shows ownership.

They're means "they are."

There means "in that place."

Both applicants were pleased with *their* interviews.

They're confident that they will be hired.

Both of them want to work *there* in the production department.

to, too, two

To shows relationship between two things.

Too means "excessively" or "also."

Two is a number.

Some people send applications *to* dozens of employers.

The career counselor suggested that sending *too* many applications is time-consuming and expensive. Knowing which companies are hiring is important, *too.*

Sometimes, sending as few as *two* applications is sufficient.

who's, whose

Whose (belonging to whom) shows ownership.

Who's means "Who is."

It's a good idea to speak with someone *whose* career parallels your job interests.

Speaking to someone *who's* in a career that interests you is a useful technique.

your, you're

You're means "you are."

Y*our* means "belonging to you."

What is it *you're* interested in studying?

What is *your* career goal?

EXERCISE 13 Homonyms and Word Pairs

Underline the correct word. Be able to tell why the word is correct.

1. It may be that (your you're) interested in the etymology of the days of the week.
2. The days of the week get (their, there, they're) names from ancient gods and heavenly bodies.
3. People long ago looked to the gods for support and (advice, advise).
4. They believed the celestial bodies (affected, effected) their lives.
5. The Vikings and the Romans were (quiet, quite) influential in naming the days.
6. In modern English, we did not (loose, lose) the names of the sun and the moon in the days of the week—Sunday and Monday.
7. (Their, They're) two days named after Viking gods.
8. A third day is named after the Viking gods, (to, too, two).
9. What is the (affect, effect) of having Tuesday, Wednesday, and Thursday named after the powerful gods: Tyr, the god of war and the sky; Woden or Odin, the chief god; and Thor, the god of thunder?
10. Friday could (have, of) been named for Frigga, the wife of Odin and goddess of love and the household.
11. Saturday gets (it's, its) name from the planet Saturn.
12. A word's etymology or history can be (quiet, quite) interesting.

EXERCISE 14 Homonyms and Word Pairs

Underline any word that is used incorrectly. Write the correct word on the line before the sentence. If there is no incorrect word in a sentence, write "correct" on the line before the sentence.

_______ 1. The original Roman calendar shows fewer days then the calendar used in the United States today.

_______ 2. The Roman calendar had 304 days, but their are usually 365 days in the modern calendar.

_______ 3. The Roman calendar started it's year with the month of March.

_______ 4. January is named for the two-headed god Janus, whose heads face the past and the future.

_______ 5. Februa, the Feast of Purification in early Rome, gives its name too the month of February.

_______ 6. The month April could of been named for Aphrodite, the Greek goddess of love and beauty.

_______ 7. The name May is taken losely from the name Maia, the Roman goddess of spring.

_______ 8. As protector and advisor of women, Juno, the queen of the gods, was honored by the month of June.

_______ 9. Those who worshipped Juno, the wife of Jupiter, believed she had a powerful effect on the other gods.

_______ 10. In 44 B.C. Julius Caesar, who is not known as a quite leader, changed the month Quintillis to Julius, or July, after himself.

_______ 11. Both Julius Caesar and another Roman leader, Augustus Caesar, wanted their names too live on in months named for themselves.

_______ 12. September, October, November, and December get there names from the Roman words for "seven," "eight," nine," and "ten," which were their places in the old Roman calendar.

ACKNOWLEDGMENTS

Permission to reprint from the following sources is gratefully acknowledged:

Pages 5-6: Reprinted with the permission of Simon & Schuster Books for Young Readers, an imprint of Simon & Schuster Children's Publishing Division from *The Lost Garden* by Laurence Yep. Copyright © 1991 by Laurence Yep.

Pages 34-36: From *Hunger of Memory* by Richard Rodriguez. Reprinted by permission of David R. Godine, Publisher, Inc. Copyright © 1982 by Richard Rodriguez.

Pages 54-56: Reprinted from *I Tell You Now: Autobiographical Essays by Native American Writers* edited by Brian Swann and Arnold Krupat by permission of the University of Nebraska Press. Copyright © 1987 by the University of Nebraska Press.

Pages 72-74: From *Mount Allegro* by Jerre Mangione, © 1981. Reprinted with permission.

Pages 96-98: *And the Bridge Is Love* by Faye Moskowitz. Copyright © 1991 by Faye Moskowitz. Reprinted by permission of Beacon Press, Boston.

Pages 124-126: Reprinted courtesy of EBONY MAGAZINE.

Pages 150-152: From *Breaking Barriers: A Memoir* by Carl Rowan. Copyright © 1991 by Carl T. Rowan. By permission of Little, Brown and Company (Inc.).

Pages 170-171: Carolyn Glenn Brewer, *Caught in the Path*, Prairie Fugure Books. Reprinted by permission of the author.

Pages 190-193: Excerpts from *Silent Dancing: A Partial Remembrance of a Puerto Rican Childhood* by Judith Ortiz Cofer are reprinted with permission from the publisher (Houston: Arte Público Press—University of Houston, 1990).

Pages 216-218: From *Sabbath: Remembering the Sacred Rhythm of Rest and Delight* by Wayne Muller. Copyright © 1999 by Wayne Muller. Used by permission of Bantam Books, a division of Random House, Inc.

INDEX